Teacher Guide

LEVEL D

VOCABULARY

word meaning, pronunciation, prefixes, suffixes, synonyms, antonyms, and fun!

in Action

LOYOLA PRESS.

Chicago

LOYOLA PRESS.

3441 N. Ashland Avenue
Chicago, Illinois 60657
(800) 621-1008
www.loyolapress.com

Cover & Interior Art: Anni Betts
Cover Design: Judine O'Shea
Interior Design: Kathy Greenholdt

Copyright © 2010 Loyola Press

Manufactured in the United States of America.

ISBN-10: 0-8294-2777-5

ISBN-13: 978-0-8294-2777-6

10 11 12 13 14 15 16 17 Hess 10 9 8 6 7 5 4 3 2 1

VISIT
www.vocabularyinaction.com
ACCESS CODE: VTB-8994

Pronunciation Key

This key shows the meanings of the abbreviations and symbols used throughout the book.

Some English words have more than one possible pronunciation. This book gives only one pronunciation per word, except when different pronunciations indicate different parts of speech. For example, when the word *relay* is used as a noun, it is pronounced rē´ lā; as a verb, the word is pronounced rə lā´.

Parts of Speech

adj.	adjective	*int.*	interjection	*prep.*	preposition
adv.	adverb	*n.*	noun	*part.*	participle
				v.	verb

Vowels

ā	tape	ə	about, circus	ôr	torn
a	map	ī	kite	oi	noise
âr	stare	i	win	ou	foul
ä	car, father	ō	toe	o͞o	soon
ē	meet	o	mop	o͝o	book
e	kept	ô	law	u	tug

Consonants

ch	check	ŋ	rang	y	yellow
g	girl	th	thimble	zh	treasure
j	jam	th̶	that	sh	shelf

Stress

The accent mark follows the syllable receiving the major stress, such as in the word *plaster* (plas´ tər).

Introduction

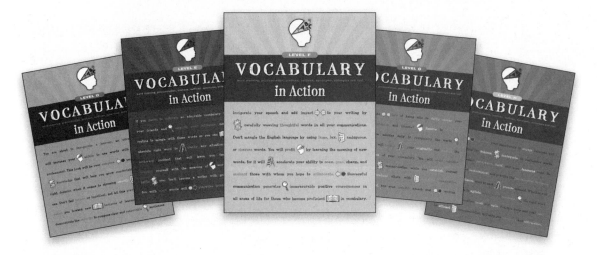

Vocabulary in Action is the premier vocabulary development program that increases students' literacy skills and improves test scores.

Researchers and educators agree that vocabulary development is essential in learning how to communicate effectively through listening, speaking, reading, and writing. The National Reading Panel (2000) has identified vocabulary as one of the five areas that increase students' reading ability. After the third grade, reading difficulties are often attributed to a vocabulary deficit—an inability to understand word meaning.

Vocabulary in Action offers the following elements to help students develop this critical literacy skill:

- Flexible leveling and student placement for individualized instruction

- Words that were researched and selected specifically for frequency, occurrence, and relevance to assessment and everyday life

- Intentional, direct instruction focused on words and their meanings, usage, and relationships to other words

- Repeated word appearance in a variety of contexts for extensive exposure and practice with literal and figurative meanings

- Application of new vocabulary skills through practice exercises, assessments, and standardized test preparation opportunities

Each Student Book includes

- **Program Pretest** to identify level of understanding

- **Research-based Word Lists** selected for frequency, occurrence, and relevance to assessment

- **One Hundred or More Related Words** including synonyms and antonyms

- **Word Pronunciations, Meanings, and Identifications of Parts of Speech**

- **At Least a Dozen Activities per Chapter**, including activities for words in context, word meaning, word usage, related words, and word building

- **Challenge Words and Activities**

- **Fun with Words** activities for additional practice

- **Test-Taking Tips** section covering test-taking skills, testing formats, and study of testing vocabulary including classic roots, prefixes, and suffixes

- **Special Features** for etymology, mnemonic devices, historical facts, word trivia, and word origin

- **Notable Quotes** that show words in context

- **Chapter Review Assessments** for multiple chapters

- **Program Posttest** to determine overall growth

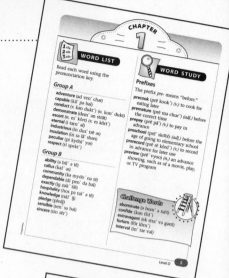

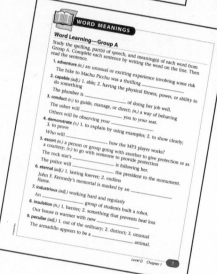

Total Vocabulary Word Count by Level

LEVEL	WORDS TO KNOW	ADDITIONAL WORDS
D	150	over 100
E	225	over 150
F, G, H	375	over 200

Each Teacher Guide includes

- **Annotated Guide** similar to the student book for easy correction

- **Additional Games and Activities** for a variety of groupings, learning styles, multiple intelligences, and levels of proficiency in English

- **Suggestions for Guided and Independent Practice**

- **Academic Language Practice** with games and activities, including work with classic roots

- **Icons** for easy identification

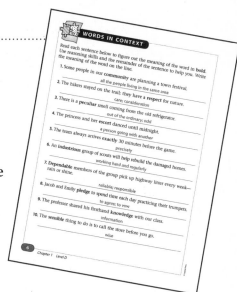

The *Vocabulary in Action* Web site includes

- Assessments

- Pretests and Reviews

- Word Lists and Definitions

- Vocabulary Games

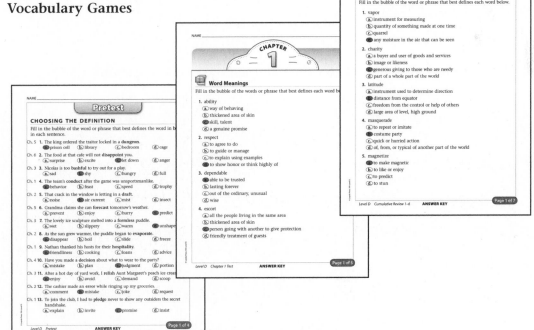

How to Implement This Program

With *Vocabulary in Action*, it is easy to differentiate instruction to meet the needs of all students.

Student Placement

Use the following chart to help determine the book most appropriate for each individual student. Differences in level include word difficulty, sentence complexity, and ideas presented in context. In addition to the chart, consider a student's achievement level on any pretest that you give. Adjust books based on a student's achievement on a pretest and other vocabulary assignments, his or her ability to retain new information, and the student's overall work ethic and interest level.

Placement Levels

Typical Grade-Level Assignments		Accelerated Grade-Level Assignments	
LEVEL	GRADE	LEVEL	GRADE
D	4	D	3
E	5	E	4
F	6	F	5
G	7	G	6
H	8	H	7

To Begin

At the beginning of the year, choose a book for each student based on the above criteria. Have each student take the program pretest in his or her book. Avoid timing the test. Give students enough time to complete the test thoughtfully and with confidence. After grading the test and noting student achievement levels, make book adjustments if necessary.

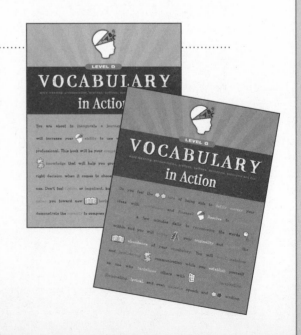

Work Through the Chapters

Follow these steps to implement each chapter.

1. **Chapter opener:** Have students work with partners, in small groups, or with you to read aloud each word in the **Word List.** Check pronunciation and discuss the definition of each word, having students find the words in a dictionary if you have time. Have students review the **Word Study** section. Introduce the **Challenge Words** in the same way as the Word List. Then have students remove the page and complete the back side.

2. **Chapter pages:** Based on students' confidence and ability, assign students to complete chapter activities independently, with you, with peers, or as homework. Students should complete activities for Words in Context, Word Meanings, Use Your Vocabulary, Word Learning, Synonyms, Antonyms, Word Study, Challenge Words, and Fun with Words. Provide support through modeling and discussion. Here are some approaches:

   • Teacher presents and completes a page with students during the first 10 or 15 minutes of each reading or language arts session. Pages are reviewed simultaneously as guided practice.

   • Students complete chapter pages in class after other reading or language arts assignments are complete. Pages are collected and reviewed after class.

   • Students complete chapter pages as homework assignments, one page per night. Pages are collected and reviewed after completion.

3. **Reteaching/additional practice:** Monitor student progress on a regular basis. If students need additional practice, use the **Games & Activities** on pages 93–98 of this guide or the **Teacher Activities** on pages 99–100.

4. **Standardized test preparation:** At least one month prior to standardized testing, work with students to complete pages 89–90.

5. **Chapter reviews:** After completing every two chapters, administer the Chapter Review to note students' progress and to identify difficult words.

6. **Assessment:** Have students complete a formal assessment after each chapter. Visit **www.vocabularyinaction.com** and access the assessment with this code: **VTB-8994.** You can also access a **Pretest** and **Review.**

Sample Yearly Plan for Level D

Following is one way to implement *Vocabulary in Action* for Level D.

WEEK	STUDENT BOOK	RELATED ACTIVITIES
1	Pretest	
2–6	Chapter 1	Games & Activities (pp. 93–98) Teacher Activities (pp. 99–100) Chapter 1 Assessment
7–11	Chapter 2	Games & Activities (pp. 93–98) Teacher Activities (pp. 99–100) Chapter 2 Assessment
12	Review Chapters 1 and 2	Online Games (www.vocabularyinaction.com) Cumulative Review
13–17	Chapter 3	Games & Activities (pp. 93–98) Teacher Activities (pp. 99–100) Chapter 3 Assessment
18–22	Chapter 4	Games & Activities (pp. 93–98) Teacher Activities (pp. 99–100) Chapter 4 Assessment
23	Review Chapters 3 and 4	Online Games (www.vocabularyinaction.com) Cumulative Review
24–28	Chapter 5	Games & Activities (pp. 93–98) Teacher Activities (pp. 99–100) Chapter 5 Assessment
29–33	Chapter 6	Games & Activities (pp. 93–98) Teacher Activities (pp. 99–100) Chapter 6 Assessment
34	Review Chapters 5 and 6	Online Games (www.vocabularyinaction.com) Cumulative Review
35	Posttest	

Pretest

This test contains some of the words you will find in this book. It will give you an idea of the kinds of words you will study. When you have completed all the chapters, the posttest will measure what you have learned.

CHOOSING THE DEFINITIONS

Fill in the bubble of the item that best defines the word in bold in each sentence.

Ch. 1   1. At night, the old house made **peculiar** sounds.
       a. loud   **b.** pleasant   **c.** familiar   **d.** strange

Ch. 4   2. A **citizen** has the right to vote.
       a. village   **b.** resident   **c.** person   **d.** woman

Ch. 5   3. From the **plateau**, we could see for miles.
       a. valley   **b.** border   **c.** highland   **d.** ocean

Ch. 3   4. The baby was **bashful** around strangers.
       a. confident   **b.** shy   **c.** silly   **d.** sly

Ch. 2   5. The crops grew tall in the **fertile** soil.
       a. rich   **b.** rocky   **c.** damp   **d.** dry

Ch. 6   6. Mr. Mendez **exaggerated** the size of the fish he caught.
       a. belittled   **b.** shouted out   **c.** measured   **d.** magnified

Ch. 1   7. The ranger shared useful **knowledge** about camping.
       a. tools   **b.** information   **c.** thoughts   **d.** rules

Ch. 2   8. Work carefully so that you will not make an **error**.
       a. mistake   **b.** answer   **c.** project   **d.** step

Ch. 3   9. The artist turned the **formless** lump of clay into a beautiful statue.
       a. hard   **b.** sculpted   **c.** heavy   **d.** unshaped

Ch. 5   10. The umpire settled the **dispute** quickly.
       a. friendship   **b.** question   **c.** argument   **d.** agreement

Ch. 6   11. Ayla did not want to **disappoint** her teammates.
       a. trust   **b.** go with   **c.** please   **d.** let down

Ch. 3   12. Sleeping late on Saturday morning is a real **luxury**.
       a. expense   **b.** extra comfort   **c.** necessity   **d.** nap

Ch. 6   13. The piano teacher played a sad **melody**.
       a. tune   **b.** story   **c.** speech   **d.** feeling

Ch. 1   **14.** The new shoes are **exactly** the right size.

     a. almost   **b.** incorrectly   **c.** precisely   **d.** not

Ch. 3   **15.** The whole family **relished** the food Dad grilled.

     a. cooked   **b.** disliked   **c.** enjoyed   **d.** served

Ch. 5   **16.** Our new puppy **whined** when we left it alone.

     a. whimpered   **b.** barked   **c.** leaped   **d.** slept

Ch. 6   **17.** The backyard was **disarranged** after the children's party.

     a. crowded   **b.** messy   **c.** empty   **d.** neat

Ch. 2   **18.** Noah started a program to **recycle** used paper at his school.

     a. throw away   **b.** haul   **c.** use again   **d.** count

Ch. 6   **19.** In her **haste** to catch the bus, Alexis forgot her lunch.

     a. fear   **b.** a heavy load   **c.** dislike   **d.** hurry

Ch. 3   **20.** Many people come to the United States to find **liberty**.

     a. gold   **b.** freedom   **c.** adventure   **d.** homes

Ch. 5   **21.** The artist placed the painting on the **easel**.

     a. frame   **b.** place   **c.** wall   **d.** stand

Ch. 4   **22.** Victoria's **ancestors** lived in Peru.

     a. sisters   **b.** family founders   **c.** grandchildren   **d.** cousins

Ch. 1   **23.** I enjoy living in our friendly **community**.

     a. apartment   **b.** neighborhood   **c.** house   **d.** country

Ch. 6   **24.** They will build a new store on the **vacant** lot.

     a. weedy   **b.** crowded   **c.** empty   **d.** large

Ch. 4   **25.** The law **forbids** skateboarding at the mall.

     a. does not allow   **b.** urges   **c.** allows   **d.** wants

Ch. 2   **26.** I thought my brother broke the game, but he was **innocent**.

     a. happy   **b.** wrong   **c.** too young   **d.** not guilty

Ch. 5   **27.** The chef prepared a **banquet** for the wedding guests.

     a. party favor   **b.** dessert   **c.** feast   **d.** snack

Ch. 1   **28.** The new girl showed great athletic **ability**.

     a. clumsiness   **b.** talent   **c.** weakness   **d.** charm

Ch. 4   **29.** My cousin is the **companion** I trust the most.

     a. teacher   **b.** doctor   **c.** teammate   **d.** friend

Pretest   Level D

Ch. 6 **30.** This medicine has a **horrid** smell.
    a. dreadful   **b.** pleasant   **c.** nice   **d.** flowery

Ch. 1 **31.** In kindergarten, we vowed that our friendship would be **eternal.**
    a. very short   **b.** important   **c.** lasting forever   **d.** ordinary

Ch. 5 **32.** The **flexible** hose easily bent around the corner.
    a. rubber   **b.** not stiff   **c.** rigid   **d.** garden

Ch. 2 **33.** It took the hikers all day to reach the bottom of the **canyon.**
    a. hill   **b.** stream   **c.** frozen ground   **d.** deep valley

Ch. 1 **34.** The teacher **demonstrated** how to stop on skis.
    a. showed   **b.** understood   **c.** recorded   **d.** learned

Ch. 3 **35.** The snow looks so bright because it **reflects** the sun's rays.
    a. blocks   **b.** dims   **c.** throws back   **d.** cools down

Ch. 4 **36.** Platinum is valuable because it is **scarce.**
    a. plentiful   **b.** beautiful   **c.** rare   **d.** old

Ch. 4 **37.** Let's **reorganize** my video game library.
    a. clean out   **b.** arrange again   **c.** fill up   **d.** close again

Ch. 6 **38.** The viceroy butterfly **masquerades** as the monarch butterfly.
    a. disguises itself   **b.** flies   **c.** has a cocoon   **d.** eats

Ch. 3 **39.** We learned all about the **geography** of Australia.
    a. animals   **b.** language   **c.** people   **d.** land

Ch. 5 **40.** The flood knocked the house off its **foundation.**
    a. driveway   **b.** base   **c.** floor   **d.** roof

Ch. 2 **41.** In an address you can **abbreviate** Massachusetts to MA.
    a. spell   **b.** leave out   **c.** shorten   **d.** divide

Ch. 1 **42.** His apology sounded **sincere** to me.
    a. real   **b.** loud   **c.** dishonest   **d.** sad

Ch. 2 **43.** The woolly **garment** felt warm but scratchy.
    a. lamb   **b.** rug   **c.** clothing   **d.** sack

Ch. 6 **44.** The climber heard an **echo** as his words bounced off the mountain.
    a. whisper   **b.** shout   **c.** song   **d.** repetition

Ch. 4 **45.** The president made a difficult **decision.**
    a. choice   **b.** agreement   **c.** argument   **d.** idea

Ch. 5 **46.** Our class saw ancient mummies and dinosaur bones at the **museum.**
  a. theater **b. exhibit hall** c. stadium d. school

Ch. 3 **47.** The insects were so tiny they were almost **invisible.**
  a. bright b. strong c. miniature **d. unseen**

Ch. 2 **48.** The **journey** through the desert was long, hot, and difficult.
  a. adventure **b. trip** c. road d. river

Ch. 4 **49.** The rich **merchant** displayed colorful rugs.
  a. trader b. farmer c. sailor d. lawyer

Ch. 4 **50.** It is hard to succeed as a **professional** musician.
  a. amateur b. part-time **c. expert** d. untrained

Ch. 2 **51.** The hair on the old bear's **snout** was turning gray.
  a. chin **b. nose and mouth** c. back and legs d. tail

Ch. 3 **52.** A careful **consumer** always compares prices.
  a. buyer b. mechanic c. producer d. reader

Ch. 6 **53.** You can buy a used computer for a **fraction** of the original cost.
  a. total b. breakdown c. explanation **d. part**

Ch. 1 **54.** The weight lifter was **capable** of lifting 400 pounds.
  a. heavy **b. able** c. unfit d. allowed to

Ch. 2 **55.** Firefighters must act quickly in an **emergency.**
  a. fire **b. crisis** c. practice d. vehicle

Ch. 3 **56.** Micah's work was **satisfactory,** so he received a small raise.
  a. bad b. difficult **c. acceptable** d. fun

Ch. 5 **57.** It takes hard work and good luck to **forecast** weather correctly.
  a. predict b. ignore c. wait for d. prepare for

Ch. 4 **58.** The long wait for tickets made the spectators **impatient.**
  a. peaceful **b. restless** c. happy d. cold

Ch. 5 **59.** You do not need to understand a computer's **operation** to use one.
  a. moving parts b. repair c. engine **d. workings**

Ch. 1 **60.** An ordinary trip to the store turned into a great **adventure.**
  a. bad weather b. vacation c. project **d. exciting experience**

CHAPTER 1

WORD LIST

Read each word using the pronunciation key.

Group A

adventure (ad ven´ chər)
capable (kā´ pə bəl)
conduct (*v.* kən dukt´) (*n.* kon´ dukt)
demonstrate (dem´ ən strāt)
escort (*n.* es´ kôrt) (*v.* es kôrt´)
eternal (i tərn´ əl)
industrious (in dus´ trē əs)
insulation (in sə lā´ shən)
peculiar (pi kyo͞ol´ yər)
respect (ri spekt´)

Group B

ability (ə bil´ ə tē)
callus (kal´ əs)
community (kə myo͞o´ nə tē)
dependable (di pen´ də bəl)
exactly (ig zak´ tlē)
hospitality (hos pə tal´ ə tē)
knowledge (näl´ ij)
pledge (pledj)
sensible (sen´ sə bəl)
sincere (sin sēr´)

WORD STUDY

Prefixes

The prefix *pre-* means "before."

precook (prē ko͞ok´) (*v.*) to cook for eating later
premature (prē mə chur´) (*adj.*) before the correct time
prepay (prē pā´) (*v.*) to pay in advance
preschool (prē´ sko͞ol) (*n.*) a school for children younger than those attending elementary school
prerecord (prē rē kôrd´) (*v.*) to record in advance for later use
preview (prē´ vyoo) (*n.*) an advance showing, such as of a movie, play, or TV program

Challenge Words

abominate (ə bom´ ə nāt)
confide (kən fīd´)
extravagant (ek stra´ və gənt)
forlorn (fôr lôrn´)
interval (in´ tər vəl)

5

Level D

■ TEACHER TIP: See page ix for suggestions on how to use this page.

Read each sentence below to figure out the meaning of the word in **bold**. Use reasoning skills and the remainder of the sentence to help you. Write the meaning of the word on the line.

1. Some people in our **community** are planning a town festival.

    all the people living in the same area

2. The hikers stayed on the trail; they have **respect** for nature.

    care; consideration

3. There is a **peculiar** smell coming from the old refrigerator.

    out of the ordinary; odd

4. The princess and her **escort** danced until midnight.

    a person going with another

5. The team always arrives **exactly** 30 minutes before the game.

    precisely

6. An **industrious** group of scouts will help rebuild the damaged homes.

    working hard and regularly

7. **Dependable** members of the group pick up highway litter every week— rain or shine.

    reliable; responsible

8. Jacob and Emily **pledge** to spend time each day practicing their trumpets.

    to agree; to vow

9. The professor shared his firsthand **knowledge** with our class.

    information

10. The **sensible** thing to do is to call the store before you go.

    wise

WORD MEANINGS

Word Learning—Group A

Study the spelling, part(s) of speech, and meaning(s) of each word from Group A. Complete each sentence by writing the word on the line. Then read the sentence.

1. **adventure** *(n.)* an unusual or exciting experience involving some risk

   The hike to Machu Picchu was a thrilling ___adventure___.

2. **capable** *(adj.)* 1. able; 2. having the physical fitness, power, or ability to do something

   The plumber is ___capable___ of doing her job well.

3. **conduct** *(v.)* to guide, manage, or direct; *(n.)* a way of behaving

   The usher will ___conduct___ you to your seat.

   Others will be observing your ___conduct___.

4. **demonstrate** *(v.)* 1. to explain by using examples; 2. to show clearly; 3. to prove

   Who will ___demonstrate___ how the MP3 player works?

5. **escort** *(n.)* a person or group going with another to give protection or as a courtesy; *(v.)* to go with someone to provide protection

   The rock star's ___escort___ is following her.

   The police will ___escort___ the president to the monument.

6. **eternal** *(adj.)* 1. lasting forever; 2. endless

   John F. Kennedy's memorial is marked by an ___eternal___ flame.

7. **industrious** *(adj.)* working hard and regularly

   An ___industrious___ group of students built a robot.

8. **insulation** *(n.)* 1. barrier; 2. something that prevents heat loss

   Our house is warmer with new ___insulation___.

9. **peculiar** *(adj.)* 1. out of the ordinary; 2. distinct; 3. unusual

   The armadillo appears to be a ___peculiar___ animal.

10. respect (v.) 1. to show honor; 2. to think highly of; (n.) 1. care; 2. consideration

We _____respect_____ the opinions of our friends.

Your _____respect_____ for other readers is appreciated in the library.

Use Your Vocabulary—Group A

Choose the word from Group A that best completes each sentence. Write the word on the line. You may use the plural form of nouns and the past tense of verbs if necessary.

Would you __1__ me to the baseball game? I'm __2__ of going to the ballpark myself, but I'd like you to go with me. Besides, I know that you will be good company and will __3__ yourself well. There are a lot of busy and __4__ vendors in the stands. I have __5__ for the peanut vendors who make their job look like fun. Let's ask the peanut man to __6__ his superduper peanut throw into the back row. That was a very __7__ over-the-shoulder, behind-the-back, peanut bag toss. I think the ice-cream vendor is using mounds of popcorn for __8__ to keep the ice cream cold on this hot day. A slow baseball game would seem __9__ if it weren't for the funny vendors. Too bad our team lost the game, but we still had a memorable __10__.

1. _____escort_____

2. _____capable_____

3. _____conduct_____

4. _____industrious_____

5. _____respect_____

6. _____demonstrate_____

7. _____peculiar_____

8. _____insulation_____

9. _____eternal_____

10. _____adventure_____

Notable Quotes

"If you once forfeit the confidence of your fellow citizens, you can never regain their **respect** and esteem. It is true that you may fool all of the people some of the time; you can even fool some of the people all of the time; but you can't fool all of the people all of the time."

—Abraham Lincoln (1809–1865), 16th president of United States

Word Learning—Group B

Study the spelling, part(s) of speech, and meaning(s) of each word from Group B. Complete each sentence by writing the word on the line. Then read the sentence.

1. **ability** *(n.)* 1. skill or talent; 2. power to perform a task

   Michael's _____ability_____ to fix cars keeps my old junker running.

2. **callus** *(n.)* thickened area of the skin

   Your tight shoes caused this _____callus_____ on your foot.

3. **community** *(n.)* all the people living in the same area

   All the neighbors helped build the park for this _____community_____.

4. **dependable** *(adj.)* 1. able to be trusted; 2. reliable; 3. responsible

   Our Citizen of the Year award goes to a very _____dependable_____ person.

5. **exactly** *(adv.)* 1. without any mistake; 2. precisely

   Place the vase of flowers _____exactly_____ in the middle of the table.

6. **hospitality** *(n.)* the friendly treatment of guests or strangers

   This restaurant is famous for its good food and _____hospitality_____.

7. **knowledge** *(n.)* 1. what a person knows; 2. information

   His _____knowledge_____ of music made the concert more interesting.

8. **pledge** *(n.)* a genuine promise; *(v.)* 1. to give as security; 2. to agree to do; 3. to vow

   I need your _____pledge_____ to help me raise the money.

   I _____pledge_____ allegiance to the flag of the United States of America.

9. **sensible** *(adj.)* 1. showing good sense or judgment; 2. wise

   It was a simple yet _____sensible_____ solution to our problem.

10. **sincere** *(adj.)* 1. honest; 2. real; 3. genuine

    Hannah made a _____sincere_____ attempt to repay the money.

Use Your Vocabulary—Group B

Choose the word from Group B that best completes each sentence. Write the word on the line. You may use the plural form of nouns and the past tense of verbs if necessary.

I made a(n) __1__ to myself to learn something new this year. There are free bowling lessons for kids in my __2__ every Saturday. I think this would be a(n) __3__ choice for me because it's easy, free, and I can use my sister's bowling ball. I hope the bowling shoes don't give me a(n) __4__ on my foot. I can count on my __5__ friend, Rosa, to bowl with me. We will be good bowling partners because we have the same __6__, though our combined __7__ of the sport does not add up to much! To be fair, Rosa does know a little bit more than I do. She knows __8__ how to keep score. I am very __9__ in my promise to work hard and learn how to do that too. But even if Rosa and I never become good bowlers, we will still enjoy the kind __10__ of the owners of the bowling alley.

1. _____ pledge _____

2. _____ community _____

3. _____ sensible _____

4. _____ callus _____

5. _____ dependable _____

6. _____ ability _____

7. _____ knowledge _____

8. _____ exactly _____

9. _____ sincere _____

10. _____ hospitality _____

Vocabulary in Action

The rules of **hospitality** in the ancient Middle East were very important. In desert climates, food and water were often scarce. Homes and villages were often built near the only water source for many miles. Strict rules arose about taking care of travelers, foreigners, and strangers. If a stranger knocked on your door and asked for food, water, or a place to sleep, you were expected to provide it. To refuse was to break a sacred code that everyone lived by.

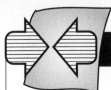

SYNONYMS

Synonyms are words that have the same or nearly the same meanings.

Part 1 Choose the word from the box that is the best synonym for each group of words. Write the word on the line.

| industrious | knowledge | respect | community | conduct |
| capable | adventure | eternal | hospitality | escort |

1. admire; consideration ⟶ respect

2. guide, direct; behavior ⟶ conduct

3. city, group, neighborhood ⟶ community

4. fit, able, competent ⟶ capable

5. everlasting, undying ⟶ eternal

6. experience, voyage, journey ⟶ adventure

7. friendliness, generosity ⟶ hospitality

8. bodyguard; go with, protect ⟶ escort

9. hardworking, busy, diligent ⟶ industrious

10. learning, information, wisdom ⟶ knowledge

Notable Quotes

"The best thing to give to your enemy is forgiveness; to an opponent, tolerance; to a friend, your heart; to your child, a good example; to a father, deference; to your mother, **conduct** that will make her proud of you; to yourself, respect; to all men, charity."

—Benjamin Franklin (1706–1790), author, inventor, statesman, founding father of United States

Part 2 Replace the underlined word(s) with a word from the box that means the same or almost the same. Write your answer on the line.

sincere	peculiar	callus	ability	insulation
pledge	sensible	demonstrate	exactly	dependable

11. His <u>skill</u> in gymnastics won him a gold medal. _____ability_____

12. The husband and wife made a <u>promise</u> to save more money.
_____pledge_____

13. The <u>lining</u> around the wire protects us from electrical shock.
_____insulation_____

14. Make each answer as <u>reasonable</u> as you can. _____sensible_____

15. Let me <u>show you</u> how to use the lawn mower. _____demonstrate_____

16. Matt cut the board <u>correctly</u> to the measurements. _____exactly_____

17. The city bus is <u>reliable</u> transportation. _____dependable_____

18. He gave us his <u>honest</u> opinion about our work. _____sincere_____

19. No one noticed the <u>odd</u> color of his hair. _____peculiar_____

20. I grip my tennis racket so tightly that I now have a <u>patch of hard skin</u> on my thumb. _____callus_____

Vocabulary in Action

The **pledge** you probably know best is the Pledge of Allegiance to the U.S. flag. This pledge was written in 1892 by Francis Bellamy. You may not know that the Pledge of Allegiance has changed a few times since it was written. The original Pledge read, "I pledge allegiance to my Flag and the Republic for which it stands: one Nation indivisible, with Liberty and Justice for all." How does that compare with today's Pledge?

ANTONYMS

Antonyms are words that have opposite or nearly opposite meanings.

> exactly   knowledge   eternal
>
> capable   sincere   ability

Part 1 Choose the word from the box that is the best antonym for each group of words. Write the word on the line.

1. false, dishonest, deceptive   *sincere*

2. weakness, incapacity   *ability*

3. ignorance, stupidity, inexperience   *knowledge*

4. sloppily, inaccurately, generally   *exactly*

5. unable, unfit   *capable*

6. passing, comes to an end, temporary   *eternal*

Part 2 Replace the underlined word with a word from the box that means the opposite or almost the opposite. Write your answer on the line.

> peculiar   industrious   dependable
>
> respect   hospitality   sensible

7. The night guard keeps <u>normal</u> working hours.   *peculiar*

8. The colonel retired from the army with <u>dishonor</u>.   *respect*

9. The welcoming committee was known for its <u>rudeness</u>.   *hospitality*

10. Kai's mother wore an <u>impractical</u> suit to the office.   *sensible*

11. The workers had an <u>idle</u> day at the factory.   *industrious*

12. Our <u>unreliable</u> washing machine began to shake.   *dependable*

WORD STUDY

Prefixes Write an answer for each statement in the space provided. Then choose a word from the box below and include it in your sentence.

> precook   premature   prepay
>
> preschool   prerecord   preview

1. Name something that you did before you started elementary school.

   _____ Write a sentence about it.

   _____ Sentence should include the word *preschool*. _____

2. Name two things you can cook to eat at a later time.

   _____   _____

   Write a sentence about one of them.

   _____ Sentence should include the word *precook*. _____

3. Name something that you can pay for in advance.

   _____ Write a sentence about it.

   _____ Sentence should include the word *prepay*. _____

4. Name two things you would like to record to watch or listen to later.

   _____   _____

   Write a sentence about one of them.

   _____ Sentence should include the word *prerecord*. _____

5. Name a movie or TV program for which you saw an advance showing.

   _____ Write a sentence about what you saw.

   _____ Sentence should include the word *preview*. _____

6. Name something that can happen too soon.

   _____ Write a sentence about it.

   _____ Sentence should include the word *premature*. _____

CHALLENGE WORDS

Word Learning—Challenge!

Study the spelling, part(s) of speech, and meaning(s) of each word. Complete each sentence by writing the word on the line. Then read the sentence.

1. **abominate** *(v.)* to hate

   People who are trying to sleep _____abominate_____ loud noises.

2. **confide** *(v.)* 1. to tell as a secret; 2. to show trust

   My best friend likes to _____confide_____ her secrets to me.

3. **extravagant** *(adj.)* 1. carelessly spending too much; 2. wasteful

   A solid gold toothbrush is an _____extravagant_____ birthday present.

4. **forlorn** *(adj.)* 1. lonely; 2. miserable; 3. hopeless; neglected

   A cat in the rain looks sad and _____forlorn_____.

5. **interval** *(n.)* a time or space between things

   There will be a 15-minute _____interval_____ between the first and second acts of the play.

Use Your Vocabulary–Challenge!

Goose on the Loose A goose wearing a diamond collar gets loose on the field during a baseball game. The players try different ways to catch it, but fail. Finally, one player has an idea that works. On a separate sheet of paper, write a news story about the incident. Use the Challenge Words above. Be sure to answer the questions *who, what, where, why,* and *when.*

> *Vocabulary in Action*
>
> A way to remember the meaning of **confide** is to think about the word *confidence,* which means "the quality or state of being certain." A person is more likely to confide in someone if he or she is certain that person can be trusted. Since the two words are so closely related, this trick may be easy to remember.

FUN WITH WORDS

The questions below use vocabulary words from this chapter. Write your answer to each question on the line.

1. Who is the person that you most *respect*? _____ Answers will vary. _____

2. Does this person live in your *community*? _____ Answers will vary. _____

3. Would you say that this person is *industrious*? Why?
Answers will vary.
_____
_____

4. What other qualities does this person *demonstrate*?
Answers will vary.
_____
_____

5. In what area might this person have a lot of *knowledge*?
Answers will vary.
_____
_____

6. What special skill or *ability* does this person have?
Answers will vary.
_____
_____

7. Do you want to be *exactly* like this person? Explain your answer.
Answers will vary.
_____
_____

8. How could you *conduct* yourself to be more like this person?
Answers will vary.
_____

CHAPTER 2

WORD LIST

Read each word using the pronunciation key.

Group A

abbreviate (ə brē´ vē āt)
capital (kap´ ət əl)
decay (di kā´)
emergency (i mər´ jən sē)
financial (fə nan´ chəl)
garment (gär´ mənt)
innocent (in´ ə sənt)
magnet (mag´ nət)
obedient (ō bē´ dē ənt)
whirl (hwərl)

Group B

canal (kə nal´)
canyon (kan´ yən)
draft (draft)
error (er´ ər)
evaporate (i vap´ ə rāt)
fertile (fərt´ l)
journey (jər´ nē)
molar (mō´ lər)
recycle (rē sī´ kəl)
snout (snout)

WORD STUDY

Suffixes

The suffix *-able* means "able to be" or "full of."

agreeable (ə grē´ ə bəl) *(adj.)* able to agree
comfortable (kəmf´ tə bəl) *(adj.)* full of comfort
enjoyable (in joi´ ə bəl) *(adj.)* full of joy
reasonable (rē´ zən ə bəl) *(adj.)* able to reason
valuable (val´ yə bəl) *(adj.)* full of value
washable (wash´ ə bəl) *(adj.)* able to be washed

Challenge Words

preside (pri zīd´)
reimburse (rē im bərs´)
tarnish (tär´ nəsh)
vagabond (vag´ ə bond)
wager (wā´ jər)

■ **TEACHER TIP:** See page ix for suggestions on how to use this page.

Read each sentence below to figure out the meaning of the word in **bold**. Use reasoning skills and the remainder of the sentence to help you. Write the meaning of the word on the line.

1. Our social studies class took a bus to the **capital** of our state to meet the governor.

   a city where a country or state's government is located

2. We are moving closer to the city so that Dad's **journey** to work won't be so long.

   travel from one place to another; a trip

3. The view from the house on the hill overlooks a **canyon**.

   deep valley

4. The best corn and soybeans are grown in the **fertile** soil of the Midwest.

   able to produce seeds, fruit, or young

5. Boatloads of people traveled on the **canal** before the railroad was built.

   human-made river

6. Who found this cute puppy with the long ears and short **snout**?

   part of an animal that contains the nose, mouth, and jaws

7. I would like my dog to be **obedient** when I command it to "sit."

   doing what one is told to do

8. Be sure to **recycle** your used newspapers, cans, and bottles.

   to process something so that it may be used again

9. My mom is now in a **financial** position to own her own business.

   relating to or dealing with money

10. Use the **magnet** to post your A+ math paper on the refrigerator.

    a piece of metal that attracts iron

WORD MEANINGS

Word Learning—Group A

Study the spelling, part(s) of speech, and meaning(s) of each word from Group A. Complete each sentence by writing the word on the line. Then read the sentence.

1. **abbreviate** *(v.)* to shorten

   When writing a letter, you may _____abbreviate_____ the title Doctor.

2. **capital** *(n.)* a city where a country or state's government is located; *(adj.)* most important

   The _____capital_____ of Texas is Austin.

   The _____capital_____ ships in the fleet were the most heavily protected.

3. **decay** *(v.)* to rot or spoil; *(n.)* a decrease in power, strength, or beauty

   As the fallen leaves _____decay_____, they make new soil.

   Bad leadership can lead to the _____decay_____ of a government's power.

4. **emergency** *(n.)* need for quick action; *(adj.)* for a time of sudden need

   The paramedics responded to the medical _____emergency_____.

   The patient was taken to the hospital's _____emergency_____ room.

5. **financial** *(adj.)* relating to or dealing with money

   Saving money can improve your _____financial_____ situation.

6. **garment** *(n.)* piece of clothing

   I want to wear a new _____garment_____ to the wedding.

7. **innocent** *(adj.)* 1. doing no wrong or evil; 2. free from guilt or blame

   The jury believed that the senator was _____innocent_____ of the crime.

8. **magnet** *(n.)* a piece of metal that attracts iron

   Anna's refrigerator is covered with souvenir _____magnets_____.

9. obedient *(adj.)* doing what one is told to do

Our old golden retriever is a loyal and _____obedient_____ dog.

10. whirl *(v.)* 1. to turn or swing in a circle; 2. to spin

We watched the merry-go-round _____whirl_____ around and around.

Use Your Vocabulary—Group A

Choose the word from Group A that best completes each sentence. Write the word on the line. You may use the plural form of nouns and the past tense of verbs if necessary.

Let's take my car for a(n) __1__ around the streets of the state __2__ . We need to be __3__ when it comes to the traffic laws. If we get stopped for a ticket, we may have to __4__ our tour, which is already too short. Let's go to the shopping district where fine __5__ are sold. It is an old part of town. Some buildings have __6__ , but there are plans to restore many of them. The old bookstores draw me in like a(n) __7__ and tempt me to spend even my __8__ funds. If we run out of cash, we'll just head to the __9__ district, where all the banks are located. I hope my wife will believe that I am __10__ of overspending.

1. _____whirl_____

2. _____capital_____

3. _____obedient_____

4. _____abbreviate_____

5. _____garments_____

6. _____decayed_____

7. _____magnet_____

8. _____emergency_____

9. _____financial_____

10. _____innocent_____

Word Learning—Group B

Study the spelling, part(s) of speech, and meaning(s) of each word from Group B. Complete each sentence by writing the word on the line. Then read the sentence.

1. **canal** *(n.)* human-made waterway

   The boats traveled between the two cities on the narrow ___canal___.

2. **canyon** *(n.)* deep valley

   The campers hiked to the bottom of the ___canyon___.

3. **draft** *(n.)* current of air; *(v.)* to make a rough copy or sketch of

   Please block the cold ___draft___ coming through the window.

   Would you edit the first ___draft___ of my essay?

4. **error** *(n.)* mistake

   Take a moment to correct the ___error___ in this paragraph.

5. **evaporate** *(v.)* to dry up or disappear

   The water will ___evaporate___ when you heat it.

6. **fertile** *(adj.)* able to produce seeds, fruit, or young

   The farmer planted a ___fertile___ field with tomatoes and beans.

7. **journey** *(n.)* 1. travel from one place to another; 2. a trip; *(v.)* to travel

   Bob and Carol are planning a ___journey___ around the world.

   They will ___journey___ through Europe, Asia, and North America.

8. **molar** *(n.)* tooth used for grinding

   Her toddler's new ___molar___ is coming in nicely.

9. **recycle** *(v.)* to process something so that it may be used again

   ___Recycle___ all the empty aluminum cans.

10. snout *(n.)* part of an animal that contains the nose, mouth, and jaws

The muzzle goes around the watchdog's _____snout_____.

Use Your Vocabulary—Group B

Choose the word from Group B that best completes each sentence. Write the word on the line. You may use the plural form of nouns and the past tense of verbs if necessary.

I took a(n) __1__ by boat through the countryside. I traveled by way of a(n) __2__. The views of green, __3__ farmlands were relaxing. I felt my worries __4__ like water on a hot day. My boat was followed for a mile or so by a sheep dog with white feet and a black __5__. His smile was so wide that I could see the __6__ at the back of his jaw. His thick fur looked to be good at keeping out the cold __7__ of winter, but I bet he was uncomfortable on this warm day. I crumpled my drink can and threw it into a bin to be __8__. I remembered then that I had almost decided to hike deep into the western __9__ on my vacation this year. That would have been a huge __10__. I needed this clear air and lazy pace to restore my energy and make me feel whole again!

1. _____journey_____
2. _____canal_____
3. _____fertile_____
4. _____evaporate_____
5. _____snout_____
6. _____molars_____
7. _____drafts_____
8. _____recycled_____
9. _____canyons_____
10. _____error_____

Vocabulary in Action

A way to remember the meaning of *error* is to think about the word *erratic*, which means "lacking consistency or uniformity." A person is more likely to make an error if his or her actions lack consistency or uniformity. Since both words begin with *err*, this trick may be easy to remember.

SYNONYMS

Synonyms are words that have the same or nearly the same meanings.

Part 1 Choose the word from the box that is the best synonym for each group of words. Write the word on the line.

obedient	error	capital	financial	canyon
magnet	innocent	emergency	recycle	garment

1. blameless, faultless, pure   _innocent_

2. crisis; suddenly needed   _emergency_

3. dress, apparel, clothing   _garment_

4. gorge, valley, ravine   _canyon_

5. important, chief, supreme   _capital_

6. metal that attracts   _magnet_

7. loyal, devoted, willing   _obedient_

8. mistake, blunder, blooper   _error_

9. money-related, economic   _financial_

10. use again   _recycle_

Notable Quotes

"The wonders of the Grand **Canyon** cannot be adequately represented in symbols of speech nor by speech itself. The resources of the graphic art are taxed beyond their powers in attempting to portray its features . . . The glories and beauties of form, color, and sound unite in the Grand Canyon."

—John Wesley Powell (1834–1902), explorer, geologist, soldier

Part 2 Replace the underlined word(s) with a word from the box that means the same or almost the same. Write your answer on the line.

journey	fertile	canal	whirl	molar
snout	decay	abbreviate	draft	evaporate

11. Gently hold Roscoe's <u>muzzle</u> closed so he'll swallow the pill.

    _____snout_____

12. The best oranges are grown in the <u>rich</u> soil of this valley.

    _____fertile_____

13. The ripe vegetables in the stalled truck began to <u>rot</u> in the hot sun. _____decay_____

14. Write state names in full; do not <u>shorten</u> them. _____abbreviate_____

15. Here's our first <u>version</u> of the script for this year's Thanksgiving Day play. _____draft_____

16. The dancers will <u>spin</u> faster as the music gets louder.

    _____whirl_____

17. Be sure to brush each <u>back tooth</u>. _____molar_____

18. Don't let your dreams <u>disappear</u> when things get difficult.

    _____evaporate_____

19. Austin showed us photographs from his <u>voyage</u> to the Great Barrier Reef. _____journey_____

20. Our barge cruise takes us through an old shipping <u>channel</u> in France.

    _____canal_____

ANTONYMS

Antonyms are words that have opposite or nearly opposite meanings.

Part 1 Choose the word from the box that is the best antonym for each group of words. Write the word on the line.

| error | canyon | abbreviate | fertile | decay |

1. peak, mountaintop, highland   _canyon_

2. correctness, accuracy   _error_

3. grow, flourish, strengthen   _decay_

4. sterile, barren, not productive   _fertile_

5. lengthen, extend, spell out   _abbreviate_

Part 2 Replace the underlined word(s) with a word from the box that means the opposite or almost the opposite. Write your answer on the line.

| draft | recycle | obedient | innocent | capital |

6. "All evidence points to the fact that this man is <u>guilty</u>," said the lawyer. _innocent_

7. The senator proclaimed the president's plan as a <u>trivial</u> idea. _capital_

8. Can anyone here <u>finalize</u> the written portion of our report? _draft_

9. The young actor was <u>defiant</u> whenever the director told him what to do. _obedient_

10. Wait! Don't <u>throw away</u> yesterday's newspapers until I've read them. _recycle_

WORD STUDY

Suffixes Write the word from the box below that best completes each of the following sentences.

> agreeable   comfortable   enjoyable
>
> reasonable   valuable   washable

1. The cotton blanket is _____washable_____, but the wool blanket is not.

2. My baseball card collection is _____valuable_____, and I'm going to sell it.

3. The committee was _____agreeable_____ to your idea and voted yes.

4. The good dinner and interesting company made for a(n) _____enjoyable_____ evening.

5. Please sit in this cozy and _____comfortable_____ chair.

6. The rule that says you must be on time for class is _____reasonable_____.

> *Vocabulary in Action*
>
> People sometimes use the word *vagabond* to mean someone who is homeless or impoverished. But the word simply refers to someone who wanders from place to place. It comes from a Latin word that means "to wander."

CHALLENGE WORDS

Word Learning–Challenge!

Study the spelling, part(s) of speech, and meaning(s) of each word below. Complete each sentence by writing the word on the line. Then read the sentence.

1. **preside** *(v.)* to hold the place of authority

   A new judge will _____preside_____ in traffic court today.

2. **reimburse** *(v.)* to pay back to someone

   Please _____reimburse_____ me five dollars for the phone calls you made.

3. **tarnish** *(v.)* 1. to dull the luster of; 2. to bring disgrace on; *(n.)* a dull coating, especially on silver

   If I'm caught committing a crime, it will _____tarnish_____ my reputation.

   You can remove the _____tarnish_____ from a silver spoon by polishing it.

4. **vagabond** *(n.)* person who moves from place to place; *(adj.)* wandering

   We call my uncle a _____vagabond_____ because he never lives in one place for long.

   The _____vagabond_____ sailor kept sailing from one continent to another.

5. **wager** *(v.)* to make a bet; *(n.)* the act of betting

   Did they _____wager_____ their money on the winner or the loser?

   If you lose this _____wager_____, it will cost you money.

Use Your Vocabulary—Challenge!

Vacation Race Bailey bets Seth that she can ride across Arizona on her bike in six weeks. If she wins, Seth will pay her expenses. On a separate sheet of paper, write a story about Bailey's trip. Use the Challenge Words above. Be sure to tell what happens during the trip and who wins the bet.

Find the 18 misspelled vocabulary words and underline them. Then spell each word correctly on the lines below the letter.

Dear Gavin,

What a week! It started with an <u>emergincy</u> meeting to talk about how to <u>recycel</u> all the farm's newspapers and cans. I made an <u>inocent</u> suggestion that no one liked, so I <u>whurled</u> out of the room. I was not paying attention as I walked down the path, and I almost fell into the <u>caynon</u>. Fortunately, my dog, Barker, was with me. He grabbed me with his <u>snaut</u> and pulled me to safety. He's such a good, <u>obediente</u> dog.

But that's not all. Tuesday the smell of <u>decaiy</u> came floating through my window with a <u>drapht</u>. I looked out to see that the water in the <u>cannal</u> had all <u>evapporated</u>. My once <u>fertil</u> garden was quickly dying. I threw on some <u>garmints</u> and rushed to buy hoses. Alas, my <u>finanshal</u> situation is not good, so I could only buy one watering can instead. I have been watering plants nonstop for three days. My arms and legs ache, and I believe even my <u>molers</u> are starting to get tired!

Perhaps it was an <u>errer</u> to move so far away from the city. I thought it was a <u>capitle</u> idea at first, but now I'm not so sure. What do you think I should do? Could you <u>jurney</u> to see me? I'd love to have you even for a few days. And I promise there will be no more disasters!

Best wishes,
Diana

emergency	canal
recycle	evaporated
innocent	fertile
whirled	garments
canyon	financial
snout	molars
obedient	error
decay	capital
draft	journey

Review 1-2

WORD MEANINGS

Fill in the bubble of the word that is best defined by each phrase.

1. odd, strange, unique
　(a.) industrious　(b.) obedient　**(c.) peculiar**　(d.) capable

2. a talent or skill
　(a.) insulation　(b.) garment　(c.) error　**(d.) ability**

3. having the power or ability to do something
　(a.) capable　(b.) fertile　(c.) financial　(d.) sensible

4. precisely, without a mistake
　(a.) exactly　(b.) sincere　(c.) dependable　(d.) emergency

5. decrease or decline in power or beauty
　(a.) evaporate　(b.) molar　(c.) recycle　**(d.) decay**

6. to make shorter
　(a.) conduct　**(b.) abbreviate**　(c.) whirl　(d.) draft

7. to make a sketch or rough copy of
　(a.) demonstrate　(b.) journey　**(c.) draft**　(d.) evaporate

8. a lowland or deep valley
　(a.) whirl　(b.) canal　**(c.) canyon**　(d.) molar

9. not guilty, doing no wrong
　(a.) innocent　(b.) industrious　(c.) dependable　(d.) capable

10. a hard place on the skin
　(a.) callus　(b.) molar　(c.) canyon　(d.) conduct

11. unending, lasting forever
　(a.) fertile　(b.) dependable　(c.) sensible　**(d.) eternal**

12. human-made waterway or river
　(a.) pledge　(b.) capital　(c.) canyon　**(d.) canal**

13. blunder, mistake
　(a.) error　(b.) molar　(c.) emergency　(d.) escort

14. a time of sudden need
　(a.) emergency　(b.) adventure　(c.) capital　(d.) community

15. having good sense or judgment
　(a.) sincere　**(b.) sensible**　(c.) obedient　(d.) industrious

SENTENCE COMPLETION

Choose the word from Part 1 that best completes each of the following sentences. Write the word in the blank. Then do the same for Part 2. You will not use all the words.

Part 1

insulation	knowledge	adventures	community
capital	garments	dependable	magnets

1. Let's listen to Harriet tell about her _____adventures_____ as a storm chaser.

2. Property taxes are the _____capital_____ item on the agenda.

3. Our _____community_____ is known for welcoming new neighbors.

4. If our home had better _____insulation_____, we could save money on our heating bills.

5. The actor's _____garments_____ looked like they were from the time of Ancient Egypt.

Part 2

sincere	journey	pledged	conduct
hospitality	demonstrated	escorted	evaporate

6. We want to _____journey_____ to Panama this summer.

7. The people of Mexico are famous for welcoming guests to their country with great _____hospitality_____.

8. The lawyers _____conduct_____ themselves in a serious way.

9. In Amsterdam, a police officer _____escorted_____ me back to the library when I got lost.

10. The students _____demonstrated_____ how oxygen is needed to keep a candle burning.

CHAPTER 3

WORD LIST

Read each word using the pronunciation key.

Group A

bashful (bash´ fəl)
charity (châr´ ə tē)
consumer (kən soo mər)
formless (fôrm´ lis)
liberty (lib´ ər tē)
luxury (luk´ shə rē)
precious (presh´ əs)
relish (rel´ ish)
satisfactory (sat is fak´ tə rē)
transport (*v.* trans pôrt´)
    (*n.* trans´ pôrt)

Group B

allegiance (ə lē ´ jəns)
chemical (kem´ i kəl)
climate (klī´ mət)
equator (i kwāt´ ər)
galaxy (gal´ ək sē)
geography (jē äg´ rə fē)
horizon (hə rī´ zən)
invisible (in viz´ ə bəl)
prey (prā)
reflect (ri flekt´)

WORD STUDY

Homophones

Homophones are words that have the same pronunciation, but a different meaning and spelling.

piece (pēs) *(n.)* one of the parts into which a thing is divided
peace (pēs) *(n.)* freedom from war

waste (wāst) *(v.)* to make poor use of; to spend uselessly
waist (wāst) *(n.)* the part of the human body between the ribs and the hips

aisle (īl) *(n.)* passage between rows of seats
isle (īl) *(n.)* a small island

Challenge Words

aroma (ə rō´ mə)
deface (di fās´)
dismantle (dis man´ təl)
enlighten (in lī´ tən)
obstinate (ob´ stə nit)

■ **TEACHER TIP:** See page ix for suggestions on how to use this page.

Read each sentence below to figure out the meaning of the word in **bold**. Use reasoning skills and the remainder of the sentence to help you. Write the meaning of the word on the line.

1. I felt **bashful** about meeting the other students in my new class.

uneasy around others; shy

2. My softball team raised money for a **charity**.

a generous giving to those who are poor, ill, or otherwise in need

3. You might think Arizona temperatures are always warm, but the winter **climate** of northern Arizona calls for coats and sweaters.

the kind of weather a place has; environment

4. My uncle, a thrifty **consumer**, always uses coupons when he shops.

a buyer and a user of goods and services

5. The freedom-loving, revolutionary statesman Patrick Henry said, "Give me **liberty** or give me death."

freedom; the right or power to do as one chooses

6. I wish I could be **invisible** so that I could sneak unseen into the opposing team's locker room and listen to their plans.

not visible; not able to be seen

7. Joshua used his birthday money to buy a **luxury** for himself—a gold-plated motorcycle with extra large tires.

extra comfort; lavishness beyond what is necessary

8. After months of being sick in bed, Jake **relished** the idea of going out.

to like or enjoy

9. Christopher Columbus believed the earth was round because he saw boats sail over the **horizon** into the morning sun.

where the earth and sky seem to meet

10. When I mixed the **chemicals** in science class, the lab filled with smoke.

a substance that may be combined with others to create new substances

WORD MEANINGS

Word Learning—Group A

Study the spelling, part(s) of speech, and meaning(s) of each word from Group A. Complete each sentence by writing the word on the line. Then read the sentence.

1. **bashful** *(adj.)* uneasy around others; shy

   The little boy flashed a _____bashful_____ grin from behind his mother.

2. **charity** *(n.)* a generous giving to those who are poor, ill, or otherwise in need

   The Salvation Army bell ringers are collecting coins for _____charity_____.

3. **consumer** *(n.)* a buyer and a user of goods and services

   A careful _____consumer_____ compares prices before buying a new car.

4. **formless** *(adj.)* having no regular form or shape

   A _____formless_____ blob is the monster in my favorite science-fiction movie.

5. **liberty** *(n.)* freedom; the right or power to do as one chooses

   The high school students have the _____liberty_____ to leave school for lunch.

6. **luxury** *(n.)* 1. extra comfort; 2. beauties of life beyond what is necessary

   Let's snuggle in the _____luxury_____ of a warm down comforter.

7. **precious** *(adj.)* of great value; cherished

   My great-grandmother's ring is a _____precious_____ family keepsake.

8. **relish** *(n.)* strong-flavored food that adds taste to other food; *(v.)* 1. to like the flavor of; 2. to like or enjoy

   Put some pickle _____relish_____ on my hot dog.

   I sure do _____relish_____ the taste of a sweet, ripe strawberry.

9. satisfactory *(adj.)* good enough to fulfill desires, hopes, demands

We didn't pass our goal, but we raised a _____satisfactory_____ amount of money for the school.

10. transport *(v.)* to carry from one place to another; *(n.)* the act of bringing something from one place to another

The truck driver said he will _____transport_____ your furniture.

The boxes shifted in the truck during the _____transport_____.

Use Your Vocabulary—Group A

Choose the word from Group A that best completes each sentence. Write the word on the line. You may use the plural form of nouns and the past tense of verbs if necessary.

Many slaves had barely enough necessities to live and didn't dream of __1__. Some people wanted to end slavery and give __2__ to the slaves. But until the Emancipation Proclamation, they could only __3__ the thought of freedom for all. The Underground Railroad, which seemed to be __4__, secretly __5__ many people to freedom in the North. One of its conductors was Harriet Tubman, who was never __6__ about speaking out against slavery. __7__ who bought Harriet Beecher Stowe's novel *Uncle Tom's Cabin* joined in supporting the antislavery movement. Once in the North, some former slaves were helped by the __8__ of those supporters until they found work. Although far from a(n) __9__ way to settle differences, the Civil War taught us that freedom was a(n) __10__ right many Americans once took for granted.

1. _____luxuries_____

2. _____liberty_____

3. _____relish_____

4. _____formless_____

5. _____transported_____

6. _____bashful_____

7. _____Consumers_____

8. _____charity_____

9. _____satisfactory_____

10. _____precious_____

Word Learning—Group B

Study the spelling, part(s) of speech, and meaning(s) of each word from Group B. Complete each sentence by writing the word on the line. Then read the sentence.

1. **allegiance** *(n.)* faithfulness or loyalty to someone or something

   It is easy to have _____allegiance_____ to a basketball team that always wins.

2. **chemical** *(n.)* a substance that may be combined with others to create new substances

   Carefully measure out the _____chemical_____ and pour it into a test tube.

3. **climate** *(n.)* the kind of weather a place has; environment

   I prefer a warm _____climate_____ where I can swim outside all year.

4. **equator** *(n.)* an imaginary circle around the middle of the earth

   The continent of Australia is south of the _____equator_____.

5. **galaxy** *(n.)* a collection of billions of stars

   The astronomer spied a distant _____galaxy_____ through her telescope.

6. **geography** *(n.)* the study of the earth's surface, climate, people, continents, and products

   To know more about earthquakes and where they happen, take a class on world _____geography_____.

7. **horizon** *(n.)* where the earth and sky seem to meet

   The cruise ship seemed to slip over the _____horizon_____ and into the setting sun.

8. **invisible** *(adj.)* not visible; not able to be seen

   Bacteria may be _____invisible_____, but they can cause visible changes to the world around us.

9. **prey** *(n.)* an animal hunted for food

   The nature film featured a lion chasing its _____prey_____.

10. reflect *(v.)* 1. to give back or throw back light, heat, or sound; 2. to send back an image or a likeness

The spy held up a mirror to _____ reflect _____ the light back into the guard's eyes.

Use Your Vocabulary—Group B

Choose the word from Group B that best completes each sentence. Write the word on the line. You may use the plural form of nouns and the past tense of verbs if necessary.

I flew across the **1** as I traveled above South America. I was headed to tropical Peru, where the **2** is warm all year. I studied the **3** of Peru before my trip and found that it has many rivers and mountains. From one of those mountaintops, I watched a beautiful sunset melt into the **4**. Then I gazed at what appeared to be an entire **5** of stars and wondered what **6** reactions could make the stars appear so bright. I heard an animal prowling nearby, probably in search of its **7**. The next day I marveled at the bright sun **8** in the glass buildings of the city of Lima. I talked with many people who were unhappy with the government. Others said that their **9** lay with their government. When it was time to leave, my jet climbed above the clouds and the now **10** city became just a pleasant memory.

1. _____ equator _____

2. _____ climate _____

3. _____ geography _____

4. _____ horizon _____

5. _____ galaxy _____

6. _____ chemical _____

7. _____ prey _____

8. _____ reflected _____

9. _____ allegiance _____

10. _____ invisible _____

Notable Quotes

"The fluttering of a butterfly's wings can effect **climate** changes on the other side of the planet."

Paul R. Ehrlich (1932–), entomologist

SYNONYMS

Synonyms are words that have the same or nearly the same meanings.

Part 1 Choose the word from the box that is the best synonym for each group of words. Write the word on the line.

charity	horizon	precious	reflect	consumer
prey	bashful	climate	relish	chemical

1. border, limit, edge   _horizon_

2. costly, dear, valuable   _precious_

3. substance, compound   _chemical_

4. compassion, kindness   _charity_

5. echo, mirror, throw back   _reflect_

6. victim, game, quarry   _prey_

7. retiring, timid, humble   _bashful_

8. flavoring, seasoning; enjoy   _relish_

9. customer, shopper, buyer   _consumer_

10. characteristic weather   _climate_

Vocabulary in Action

The **equator** is a line around the earth. It divides the earth into the Northern and Southern Hemispheres. It crosses the continents of South America and Africa as well as many islands in the Indian and Pacific Oceans. In most parts of the world, the number of hours of daytime and nighttime changes with the seasons. In places along the equator, daytime and nighttime are always 12 hours long. In fact, the word *equator* comes from a phrase that means "circle equalizing day and night."

Part 2 Replace the underlined word(s) with a word from the box that means the same or almost the same. Write your answer on the line.

> liberty   transport   geography   galaxy   formless
> satisfactory   allegiance   invisible   equator   luxury

11. The workers were asked for their complete <u>devotion</u> to the company.
    _____allegiance_____

12. Our solar system is a very small part of a large <u>star cluster</u>.
    _____galaxy_____

13. Julia's old car may not be fast, but it provides <u>adequate</u> transportation.
    _____satisfactory_____

14. We will need a very large truck to <u>move</u> everything at once.
    _____transport_____

15. As the fog rolled in, the airport was <u>out of sight</u> to the incoming
    planes. _____invisible_____

16. The revolutionary soldiers demanded <u>freedom</u> for their captured
    comrades. _____liberty_____

17. Next year's clothing fashions will feature a <u>shapeless</u> sort of dress.
    _____formless_____

18. Some expensive hotels provide the <u>special pleasure</u> of fresh flowers in
    each room. _____luxury_____

19. Somewhere in Africa, tourists can stand with one foot on each side of
    the <u>imaginary line that divides the earth</u>. _____equator_____

20. My new atlas has maps that show the <u>land formations</u> of each
    country. _____geography_____

Antonyms are words that have opposite or nearly opposite meanings.

Part 1 Choose the word from the box that is the best antonym for each group of words. Write the word on the line.

luxury	allegiance	invisible
reflect	liberty	formless

1. slavery, dependence, captivity   _liberty_

2. absorb, take in   _reflect_

3. shaped, geometric, rigid   _formless_

4. basic, necessity, requirement   _luxury_

5. disloyalty, treason, betrayal   _allegiance_

6. seen, obvious, in view   _invisible_

Part 2 Replace the underlined word with a word from the box that means the opposite or almost the opposite. Write your answer on the line.

precious	charity	consumer
bashful	relish	satisfactory

7. The young man entered the office in a <u>bold</u> manner.
bashful

8. As a <u>producer</u> of baked goods, he found he had trouble losing weight.
consumer

9. Makayla and Molly <u>dislike</u> the idea of getting up early each morning for band practice. _relish_

10. Some said the ballplayer appeared merely for the publicity; others called it an act of <u>greed</u>. _charity_

11. Trevor's power tools are <u>useless</u> for this job. _satisfactory_

12. Grandmother's old furniture is <u>worthless</u> to me. _precious_

39

WORD STUDY

Homophones Write the homophones from the box below on the lines to complete what each person said.

> piece   peace   waste   waist   aisle   isle

1. The bride said, "After I walk down the church _____aisle_____ with my groom, we will honeymoon on a small Caribbean _____isle_____."

2. The party guest said, "I don't want to _____waste_____ any of my dinner, but if I eat all of this, I won't be able to button my jacket around my _____waist_____."

3. The pastry chef said, "I won't get any _____peace_____ around here until I give each customer a(n) _____piece_____ of my famous apple pie."

CHALLENGE WORDS

Word Learning–Challenge!

Study the spelling, part(s) of speech, and meaning(s) of each word below. Complete each sentence by writing the word on the line. Then read the sentence.

1. **aroma** *(n.)* a fragrance

   The _____aroma_____ of baking bread makes my mouth water.

2. **deface** *(v.)* to damage; to spoil the appearance of

   If you _____deface_____ this door with spray paint, you'll be punished.

3. **dismantle** *(v.)* 1. to pull down; 2. to take something apart

   We must _____dismantle_____ the dollhouse and put the pieces away.

4. enlighten *(v.)* 1. to make clear; 2. to inform; 3. to instruct

Please _____ *enlighten* _____ me of your whereabouts.

5. obstinate *(adj.)* stubborn; not giving in

This _____ *obstinate* _____ mule refuses to move from the middle of the road.

Use Your Vocabulary—Challenge!

Eyewitness to History Choose a time in history when a war was fought. Imagine that you are there shortly after an important battle. On a separate sheet of paper, write an eyewitness account of the scene. Use the Challenge Words below. Be sure the reader knows which time in history you chose.

| aroma | deface | dismantle | enlighten | obstinate |

FUN WITH WORDS

Unscramble the vocabulary words in each group. Write the words in the blanks. Then draw a line from each unscrambled word to its definition.

Group 1

1. uuxrly   _____ luxury   • an animal hunted for food

2. blisivine   _____ invisible   • beyond what is necessary

3. zoniroh   _____ horizon   • not able to be seen

4. calimech   _____ chemical   • a substance that may be combined with others to create new substances

5. rype   _____ prey   • where the earth and sky seem to meet

Group 2

1. tlecfre   _____ reflect _____   • an imaginary circle around the middle of the earth

2. quetroa   _____ equator _____   • a collection of billions of stars forming one system

3. ctialme   _____ climate _____   • study of the earth's land, climate, people, and products

4. lyxaga   _____ galaxy _____   • to send back an image

5. phragyoge   _____ geography _____   • the kind of weather a place has

Group 3

1. liglencaae   _____ allegiance _____   • to carry from one place to another

2. sprtaotnr   _____ transport _____   • faithfulness or loyalty to someone or something

3. eishlr   _____ relish _____   • uneasy around others

4. soncumre   _____ consumer _____   • a buyer and a user of goods and services

5. flubash   _____ bashful _____   • to like the taste of

Group 4

1. aiaorytfsstc   _____ satisfactory _____   • good enough to fulfill desires, hopes, and demands

2. yrthaic   _____ charity _____   • of great value

3. trebily   _____ liberty _____   • a generous giving to those who are poor, sick, or helpless

4. slemfors   _____ formless _____   • the right or power to do as one pleases

5. suoicerp   _____ precious _____   • having no regular shape

CHAPTER 4

WORD LIST

Read each word using the pronunciation key.

Group A

capacity (kə pas´ ə tē)
compare (kəm pâr´)
decision (di sizh´ ən)
difference (dif´ ər əns)
forbid (fər bid´)
impatient (im pā´ shənt)
objection (ob jek´ shən)
reflection (ri flek´ shən)
reorganize (rē ôr´ gə nīz)
scarce (skârs)

Group B

ancestor (an´ ses tər)
citizen (sit´ ə zən)
companion (kəm pan´ yən)
manufacturer (man yə fak´ chər ər)
merchant (mər´ chənt)
minister (min´ is tər)
orphan (ôr´ fən)
professional (prə fesh´ ən əl)
surgeon (sər´ jən)
usher (ush´ ər)

WORD STUDY

Analogies

An analogy is a comparison between different things. Read and study the following analogies.

Yellow is to **lemon** as **green** is to **celery.**

Ink is to **pen** as **paint** is to **brush.**

Bee is to **hive** as **bird** is to **nest.**

Challenge Words

alter (ôl´ tər)
bisect (bī´ sekt)
boycott (boi´ kot)
curtail (kər tāl´)
sequel (sē´ kwəl)

■ **TEACHER TIP:** See page ix for suggestions on how to use this page.

WORDS IN CONTEXT

Read each sentence below to figure out the meaning of the word in **bold**. Use reasoning skills and the remainder of the sentence to help you. Write the meaning of the word on the line.

1. The clothing **merchant** on Wolcott Street sold me this wool coat.

   a person who buys or sells goods for a living

2. You will have trouble finding what you want because ripe tomatoes are **scarce** in winter.

   hard to find or get; rare

3. The young kitten was an **orphan** after its mother ran away.

   a young animal without a mother

4. My mother said it was time to **reorganize** my closet, which was stuffed with piles of clothes and toys.

   to organize or form again; to arrange in a new way

5. As we hiked past Crater Lake, I saw our **reflection** in the water.

   the throwing back of rays; image or likeness

6. The woman explained that her little dog is her **companion** and goes with her everywhere.

   one who spends time with another

7. The **usher** said, "Watch your step" as he showed me to my seat.

   one who leads people to their seats in a church or public hall

8. As we looked at old photographs of our family, my father told me about our **ancestor** from Japan.

   relative who lived a long time ago

9. The **impatient** man honked his car horn and yelled, "Get moving!"

   not willing to wait or bear delay

10. My sister and her fiancé met with a **minister** to pick a wedding date.

    a member of the clergy serving in a church

WORD MEANINGS

Word Learning—Group A

Study the spelling, part(s) of speech, and meaning(s) of each word from Group A. Complete each sentence by writing the word on the line. Then read the sentence.

1. capacity *(n.)* the largest amount something can hold

The bucket is filled to _____ capacity _____ and is spilling over.

2. compare *(v.)* to note what is alike and what is different

I was asked to _____ compare _____ three spaghetti sauces and choose the best one.

3. decision *(n.)* a judgment reached

Listen to both sides of an argument before you make a

_____ decision _____.

4. difference *(n.)* characteristic that distinguishes one thing from another

Even though both vases were made by the same person, there is a great

_____ difference _____ between them.

5. forbid *(v.)* 1. to not allow; 2. to make a rule against

Christopher's parents _____ forbid _____ him to go to a movie on a school night.

6. impatient *(adj.)* 1. not willing to wait or bear delay; 2. short of temper due to irritation

Waiting for the movie to start, the children were _____ impatient _____.

7. objection *(n.)* 1. disapproval of something; 2. argument against something

The mayor raised an _____ objection _____ to the reporter's question.

8. reflection *(n.)* 1. the throwing back of rays; 2. image or likeness

She glanced at her _____ reflection _____ in the mirror.

9. reorganize *(v.)* 1. to organize or form again; 2. to arrange in a new way

I need to _____reorganize_____ my locker so that I can find my books more quickly.

10. scarce *(adj.)* hard to find or get; rare

The geologist finally found the _____scarce_____ minerals.

Use Your Vocabulary—Group A

Choose the word from Group A that best completes each sentence. Write the word on the line. You may use the plural form of nouns and the past tense of verbs if necessary.

Doctor Daedelus said, "Fill the beaker to __1__ with the bubbling potion."

"No," his patient, Ichabod, replied. "I __2__ you to do any more painful experiments on me."

"Look at your __3__ in this mirror," Doctor Daedelus said. "__4__ your new looks to this old photograph of you. Can't you see how much better you look?"

"The only __5__ I see," Ichabod said, "is in my hair."

"But, Ichabod, little by little the experiment will __6__ your facial features," Doctor Daedelus said. "In fact, this photo has helped me make a(n) __7__. Let's move your eyebrows closer to your ears!"

"No, Doctor," Ichabod protested. "I must raise a(n) __8__. My eyebrows are just fine where they are."

"Careful, Ichabod! Do not spill any of the potion from the beaker. It is __9__, and I may not be able to get more."

In a(n) __10__ voice, Ichabod exclaimed, "Oh, Doctor! I've had enough of your foolish work! I quit!"

1. _____capacity_____
2. _____forbid_____
3. _____reflection_____
4. _____Compare_____
5. _____difference_____
6. _____reorganize_____
7. _____decision_____
8. _____objection_____
9. _____scarce_____
10. _____impatient_____

Word Learning—Group B

Study the spelling, part(s) of speech, and meaning(s) of each word from Group B. Complete each sentence by writing the word on the line. Then read the sentence.

1. **ancestor** *(n.)* relative who lived a long time ago

   I was amazed to learn that my _____ancestor_____ was a queen.

2. **citizen** *(n.)* member of a nation

   Pierre, our foreign-exchange student, is a _____citizen_____ of France.

3. **companion** *(n.)* one who spends time with another

   Ashley is my _____companion_____ on long walks through the woods.

4. **manufacturer** *(n.)* a person or company whose business is to make something by hand or machine

   Haley's company is a _____manufacturer_____ of stuffed animals.

5. **merchant** *(n.)* a person who buys or sells goods for a living; *(adj.)* trading

   The jewelry _____merchant_____ is offering a discount on gold earrings.

   These _____merchant_____ ships once transported spices.

6. **minister** *(n.)* a member of the clergy serving in a church; *(v.)* to work and care for

   The congregation followed the _____minister_____ into the church.

   Hospital chaplains _____minister_____ to those who are sick.

7. **orphan** *(n.)* 1. a child whose parents are no longer living; 2. a young animal without a mother

   Thomas became an _____orphan_____ at the age of 16.

8. **professional** *(n.)* an expert in a particular field, such as law, medicine, or teaching; *(adj.)* having something to do with a job requiring special education

   Don't try to paint the car yourself; call a _____professional_____.

   The architect gave us her _____professional_____ opinion.

9. surgeon *(n.)* doctor who performs operations

They were called in to discuss the operation with the

_____surgeon_____.

10. usher *(n.)* one who leads people to their seats in a church or public hall; *(v.)* to show the way to

She took the arm of the _____usher_____ and walked into the theater.

"Who will _____usher_____ me to my box seat?" asked the movie critic.

Use Your Vocabulary—Group B

Choose the word from Group B that best completes each sentence. Write the word on the line. You may use the plural form of nouns and the past tense of verbs if necessary.

I recently traced my family tree because I plan to write a book about my **1**. To begin the search, my traveling **2** and I went to Chicago, New York, and London to look at documents about my family. I found that many of my relatives were **3** with jobs in medicine, such as my great-grandfather who was a well-known heart **4**. My great-uncle, a fur **5**, lost his store in the great Chicago Fire of 1871. After the fire, he opened a factory and became a(n) **6** of fire hoses. Another relative worked as a(n) **7** at the famous Radio City Music Hall in New York City. One of my second cousins became a(n) **8** when her parents died in the World War II bombing of London. She then moved to New York to live with the family of a **9**. After a few years in the United States, she gave up her ties to England and became a U.S. **10**.

1. _____ancestors_____

2. _____companion_____

3. _____professionals_____

4. _____surgeon_____

5. _____merchant_____

6. _____manufacturer_____

7. _____usher_____

8. _____orphan_____

9. _____minister_____

10. _____citizen_____

SYNONYMS

Synonyms are words that have the same or nearly the same meanings.

Part 1 Choose the word from the box that is the best synonym for each group of words. Write the word on the line.

scarce	surgeon	citizen	orphan	capacity
professional	reflection	usher	companion	compare

1. doctor, specialist   surgeon

2. rare, uncommon   scarce

3. relate, liken, match   compare

4. friend, mate, partner   companion

5. member of a state, national   citizen

6. limit, volume, size   capacity

7. expert, specially trained person   professional

8. guide, escort; lead, conduct   usher

9. copy, image, echo   reflection

10. parentless child, foundling   orphan

Vocabulary in Action

The word **companion** comes to us from Latin. The first part of the word, *com,* means "with." The second part comes from the Latin *panis,* which means "bread." So the word *companion* could be said to mean "with bread" or "bread buddy." This refers to the fact that someone you shared bread with was probably a friend or companion. The word first appeared in the English language at the end of the 13th century or the beginning of the 14th century.

Part 2 Replace the underlined word with a word from the box that means the same or almost the same. Write your answer on the line.

> objection forbid decision impatient difference
> merchant ancestors reorganize manufacturer minister

11. Kilkenny Castle was the ancient home of Mr. Butler's <u>forebears</u>.

    _____ancestors_____

12. The <u>judgment</u> of the football referees will be final. _____decision_____

13. The <u>contrast</u> between the students amazes me. _____difference_____

14. Waiting for the play to begin, Paige was so <u>restless</u> that she could

    hardly sit in her seat. _____impatient_____

15. The police will <u>prevent</u> reporters from entering the crime scene.

    _____forbid_____

16. The <u>storekeeper</u> offered a summer job to anyone who wanted to sell

    ice cream. _____merchant_____

17. Mr. Smith made his fortune as a <u>maker</u> of steel. _____manufacturer_____

18. The <u>preacher</u> will speak after the choir sings. _____minister_____

19. Is there any <u>argument</u> you would like to present to the student council?

    _____objection_____

20. Students will <u>rearrange</u> all the library books. _____reorganize_____

Notable Quotes

"There is no king who has not had a slave among his
ancestors, and no slave who has not had a king among his."

—Helen Keller (1880–1968), author, activist

ANTONYMS

Antonyms are words that have opposite or nearly opposite meanings.

Part 1 Choose the word from the box that is the best antonym for each group of words. Write the word on the line.

forbid	decision	difference	objection	ancestor

1. children, descendant, offspring   _____ancestor_____

2. encourage, approve   _____forbid_____

3. agreement, approval   _____objection_____

4. unity, likeness, similarity   _____difference_____

5. no opinion, hesitation   _____decision_____

Part 2 Replace the underlined word with a word from the box that means the opposite or almost the opposite. Write your answer on the line.

scarce	citizens	professional	impatient

6. Our coach gets <u>calm</u> whenever the team falls behind.
   _____impatient_____

7. All <u>visitors</u> are expected to follow the laws of this country.
   _____citizens_____

8. The weather is responsible for the <u>plentiful</u> crop this spring.
   _____scarce_____

9. The new TV channel broadcasts <u>amateur</u> sports. _____professional_____

> *Vocabulary in Action*
>
> The prefix *im-* is a variation of *in-*, which means "not." Therefore, *impatient* means "not patient." Other variations of *in-* include *il-* and *ir-*.

WORD STUDY

Analogies Complete each analogy with a word from the box.

> merchant   minister   forbid   ancestor   surgeon

1. **School** is to **principal** as **church** is to _____minister_____.
2. **Athlete** is to **football player** as **doctor** is to _____surgeon_____.
3. **Patient** is to **dentist** as **customer** is to _____merchant_____.
4. **Permit** is to **allow** as **prevent** is to _____forbid_____.
5. **Father** is to **parent** as **great-grandfather** is to _____ancestor_____.

CHALLENGE WORDS

Word Learning—Challenge!

Study the spelling, part(s) of speech, and meaning(s) of each word. Complete each sentence by writing the word on the line. Then read the sentence.

1. **alter** *(v.)* to make or become different; to change

   I need to _____alter_____ these pants to make them shorter.

2. **bisect** *(v.)* to divide into two usually equal parts

   You can _____bisect_____ a 30-degree angle into two 15-degree angles.

3. **boycott** *(v.)* to join together and refuse to buy from or associate with; *(n.)* the act of boycotting

   We will _____boycott_____ this store because they pay low wages.

   Our _____boycott_____ of the store ended when the owners agreed to pay their workers more money.

4. **curtail** *(v.)* 1. to cut short; 2. to stop part of

   We had to _____curtail_____ the game and go home early because of rain.

5. sequel *(n.)* a complete story continuing an earlier one with the same characters

The _____sequel_____ to the movie was even better than the first!

Use Your Vocabulary—Challenge!

The New Relative You discover a long-lost relative who once led a boycott. This relative also writes books and draws floor plans for houses. Imagine that you interview this fascinating person. On a separate sheet of paper, write your interview using the Challenge Words below. Be sure to tell who the relative is and where and when the interview took place.

alter	bisect	boycott	curtail	sequel

FUN WITH WORDS

Use the clues to complete the puzzle on page 54. Choose from the words in the box.

capacity	decision	merchant	reorganize
companion	forbid	minister	scarce
compare	manufacturer	orphan	surgeon

Across

1. person who buys or sells goods for a living
2. one who goes with another
3. hard to find
6. child whose parents are no longer living
8. largest amount something can hold
9. to arrange in a new way
10. doctor who performs operations
11. to not allow

Down

1. person whose business is to make something by hand or machine

4. to note what is alike and what is different among

5. a judgment reached

7. to be of service; to work and care for

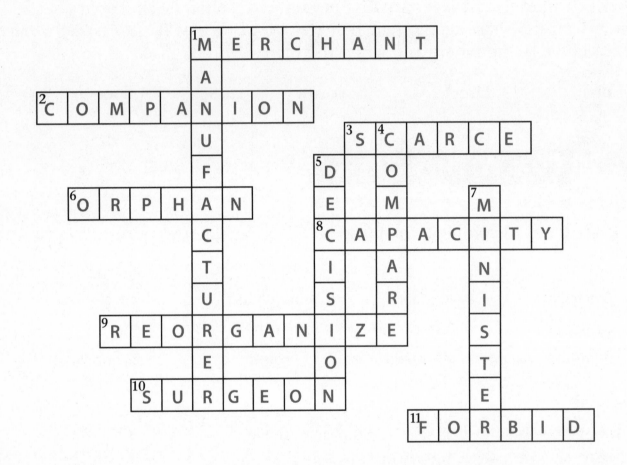

Notable Quotes

"An individual's self-concept is the core of his personality. It affects every aspect of human behavior: the ability to learn, the **capacity** to grow and change."

—Dr. Joyce Brothers (1928–), psychologist, advice columnist

Review 3-4

WORD MEANINGS

Fill in the bubble of the word that is best defined by each phrase.

1. easily embarrassed
   a. impatient **b. bashful** c. precious d. invisible

2. weather in a particular place
   a. liberty b. capacity **c. climate** d. citizen

3. giving to those who are poor, ill, or otherwise in need
   a. charity b. luxury c. objection d. merchant

4. worth a great deal
   a. formless b. impatient c. bashful **d. precious**

5. a devotion to someone or something
   a. allegiance b. reflection c. decision d. geography

6. to make a rule that does not allow
   a. compare **b. forbid** c. minister d. relish

7. one who buys and uses goods and services
   a. ancestor **b. consumer** c. surgeon d. orphan

8. to throw back light
   a. reflect b. transport c. relish d. reorganize

9. an expert in a particular job
   a. companion b. galaxy c. consumer **d. professional**

10. one who makes things for a living
    a. consumer b. prey **c. manufacturer** d. surgeon

11. not willing to put up with something
    a. impatient b. formless c. professional d. invisible

12. the amount something can hold when full
    a. charity **b. capacity** c. luxury d. decision

13. to arrange again
    a. transport b. forbid **c. reorganize** d. reflect

14. something that flavors food
    a. luxury b. prey c. horizon **d. relish**

15. one who guides
    a. merchant **b. usher** c. companion d. citizen

SENTENCE COMPLETION

Choose the word from Part 1 that best completes each of the following sentences. Write the word in the blank. Then do the same for Part 2. You will not use all the words.

Part 1

citizen	surgeon	equator	horizon
merchant	companion	scarce	liberty

1. When I became a(n) _____citizen_____ of this country, I pledged my loyalty to the United States.

2. The _____equator_____ is an imaginary line around the center of the earth.

3. We tried to find a black one, but the supply was _____scarce_____.

4. A(n) _____surgeon_____ must always scrub his or her hands and put on gloves before performing an operation.

5. My twin sister is my constant _____companion_____. We do everything together.

Part 2

transports	formless	prey	chemical
galaxy	satisfactory	decision	compares

6. I received a(n) _____satisfactory_____ grade in Spanish after completing my final exam.

7. My cat's favorite _____prey_____ are mice from the fields behind our house.

8. My friend the truck driver _____transports_____ goods from Georgia all the way to Alaska.

9. Do not use that _____chemical_____ to clean with; it is dangerous!

10. Luke finally made a(n) _____decision_____ and ordered the silver one.

CHAPTER 5

WORD LIST

Read each word using the pronunciation key.

Group A

batch (bach)
desirable (di zī′ rə bəl)
flexible (flek′ sə bəl)
forecast (fôr′ kast)
gauge (gāj)
gland (gland)
paralyze (pâr′ ə līz)
plateau (pla tō′)
vapor (vā′ pər)
whine (wīn)

Group B

bacteria (bak tir′ ē ə)
banquet (bāŋ′ kwit)
defrost (di frost′)
dispute (di spyo͞ot′)
dungeon (dun′ jən)
easel (ē′ zəl)
foreign (fôr′ in)
foundation (foun dā′ shən)
museum (myo͞o zē′ əm)
operation (op ə rā′ shən)

WORD STUDY

Suffixes

The suffix *-ward* means "in the direction of."

skyward (skī′ wərd) *(adv.)* toward the sky
backward (bak′ wərd) *(adv.)* toward the back
homeward (hōm′ wərd) *(adv.)* toward home
upward (up′ wərd) *(adv.)* toward a higher place
downward (doun′ wərd) *(adv.)* toward a lower place
westward (west′ wərd) *(adv.)* toward the west

Challenge Words

economical (e kə nom′ i kəl)
fathom (fath′ əm)
morose (mə rōs′)
perjure (pər′ jər)
refuge (ref′ yo͞oj)

57

WORDS IN CONTEXT

Read each sentence below to figure out the meaning of the word in **bold**. Use reasoning skills and the remainder of the sentence to help you. Write the meaning of the word on the line.

1. Lauren was able to **defrost** her frozen dinner in the microwave oven.

   to remove ice or frost from; to thaw

2. The scientists observed **bacteria** under a high-powered microscope.

   tiny, living things that can only be seen through a microscope

3. From where they were standing on the **plateau**, the explorers could see the land for miles.

   a large area of level, high ground

4. Daniel used a tape measure to **gauge** the distance between the bases on the field.

   to measure precisely; to estimate

5. The **museum** was fun to visit and a great place to learn more about history.

   a building in which a collection of objects is kept and displayed

6. Once he returned to the United States, Hunter discovered that he couldn't buy anything with the **foreign** money left in his pocket.

   of, from, or typical of another part of the world

7. Juan made a **batch** of oatmeal cookies for the neighborhood picnic.

   a quantity of something made at one time

8. The living conditions in the deep, dark **dungeon** were terrible, but the prisoner had no chance to escape.

   a dark, underground prison cell

9. Because so many people came to the **banquet**, the chefs ran out of food.

   a big, formal meal; a feast

10. We can settle this height **dispute** if Natalie would stand up straight.

    a quarrel

WORD MEANINGS

Word Learning—Group A

Study the spelling, part(s) of speech, and meaning(s) of each word from Group A. Complete each sentence by writing the word on the line. Then read the sentence.

1. **batch** *(n.)* a quantity of something made at one time

   Let's buy flour, butter, sugar, and chocolate chips and make a

   _____**batch**_____ of cookies.

2. **desirable** *(adj.)* 1. worth wanting or doing; 2. worth having; 3. pleasing

   For a fan of the newest video games, a high-powered computer is most

   _____**desirable**_____.

3. **flexible** *(adj.)* bendable; not stiff

   My _____**flexible**_____ fishing rod bent with the weight of the big fish.

4. **forecast** *(v.)* to predict or tell beforehand

   What do they _____**forecast**_____ for tomorrow's weather?

5. **gauge** *(v.)* 1. to measure precisely; 2. to estimate; *(n.)* an instrument for measuring or testing

   A good driver will _____**gauge**_____ a safe distance between his or her car and the car in front.

   The gas _____**gauge**_____ reads nearly empty on my mom's car.

6. **gland** *(n.)* a body organ that makes and gives out some substance

   Just the thought of chocolate cream pie makes my salivary

   _____**glands**_____ work overtime.

7. **paralyze** *(v.)* 1. to make helpless or unable to move; 2. to stun

   This drug will _____**paralyze**_____ the gorilla long enough so the vet can pull his bad tooth.

8. plateau *(n.)* a large area of level, high ground

Brad and Nicolas climbed to the level ground of the ____plateau____.

9. vapor *(n.)* 1. any moisture in the air that can be seen; 2. steam, mist, or fog

A machine used on movie sets creates water ____vapor____ for an eerie atmosphere.

10. whine *(v.)* to complain in a childish and annoying way; *(n.)* a long, high-pitched sound

If you ____whine____ about getting your dessert once more, there will be none served.

The steady ____whine____ of the jet engines made talking impossible.

Use Your Vocabulary—Group A

Choose the word from Group A that best completes each sentence. Write the word on the line. You may use the plural form of nouns and the past tense of verbs if necessary.

Kaylee put the bag with the the last __1__ of cookies into her backpack and called to her mom, "We better hurry if we want to hike to the top of the __2__ and back before sunset." Her mom came in and said, "The weather report __3__ rain today. Do you still want to go?" Kaylee __4__ the situation as she felt the __5__ in her neck, and said, "My throat is a little sore, but I won't __6__. Let's go." __7__ hung over the valley as Kaylee's mom drove in the predawn hours. Suddenly, a deer leapt into the road and seemed __8__ by the headlights before it ran away. "It is really pretty at this time," Kaylee's mom said. "I'm glad you were __9__ and decided to go." Kaylee said, "I am too. This is much more __10__ than just watching TV."

1. ____batch____

2. ____plateau____

3. ____forecasts____

4. ____gauged____

5. ____glands____

6. ____whine____

7. ____Vapor____

8. ____paralyzed____

9. ____flexible____

10. ____desirable____

Word Learning—Group B

Study the spelling, part(s) of speech, and meaning(s) of each word from Group B. Complete each sentence by writing the word on the line. Then read the sentence.

1. **bacteria** *(n.)* tiny, living things that can be seen only through a microscope

   Sickness can be spread by _____bacteria_____ on unwashed hands.

2. **banquet** *(n.)* 1. a big, formal meal; 2. a feast

   When Mrs. Deal retired after 50 years of service, the company held a _____banquet_____ in her honor.

3. **defrost** *(v.)* 1. to remove ice or frost from; 2. to thaw

   A few days before Thanksgiving is a good time to _____defrost_____ the frozen turkey.

4. **dispute** *(v.)* 1. to argue or discuss; 2. to debate; *(n.)* a quarrel

   I will _____dispute_____ your idea that it's my turn to dust.

   Erik and Zoe flipped a coin to settle their _____dispute_____ over who will clean the bathroom.

5. **dungeon** *(n.)* a dark, underground prison cell

   As part of the castle tour, we inched down narrow steps to see the _____dungeon_____.

6. **easel** *(n.)* a stand for displaying or holding a picture

   The painter displayed his finished painting on the wooden _____easel_____.

7. **foreign** *(adj.)* of, from, or typical of another part of the world

   Martin needs a passport to leave the United States and travel to _____foreign_____ countries.

8. **foundation** *(n.)* the base on which something stands

   The workers need to first lay bricks to make the _____foundation_____ for the new house.

9. **museum** (n.) a building in which a collection of objects is kept and displayed

This _____museum_____ has paintings from around the world.

10. **operation** (n.) the way something works

The detailed pictures of the inside helped me understand the _____operation_____ of a toaster.

Use Your Vocabulary—Group B

Choose the word from Group B that best completes each sentence. Write the word on the line. You may use the plural form of nouns and the past tense of verbs if necessary.

When our class went to an art **1**, the tour started on the dark lower level of the huge stone building. It felt a bit like a deep, dark **2**. Inside the galleries, though, bright lights shone on colorful paintings. There were paintings and sculptures by American and **3** artists. I liked the one that showed a lot of people feasting at a huge **4**. Two others showed a scientist looking at **5** under a microscope and an artist painting a picture at his **6**. Another showed a sagging building whose brick **7** was crumbling. One painting of a snowstorm made me feel so cold that I said I needed to go somewhere warm to **8**. Another painting showed doctors performing a brain **9**. I thought it was great, but my friends **10** me. They didn't like the painting at all.

1. _____museum_____

2. _____dungeon_____

3. _____foreign_____

4. _____banquet_____

5. _____bacteria_____

6. _____easel_____

7. _____foundation_____

8. _____defrost_____

9. _____operation_____

10. _____disputed_____

Notable Quotes

"The first rule of any technology used in a business is that automation applied to an efficient **operation** will magnify the efficiency. The second is that automation applied to an inefficient operation will magnify the inefficiency."

—Bill Gates (1955–), co-founder of Microsoft, philanthropist

SYNONYMS

Synonyms are words that have the same or nearly the same meanings.

Part 1 Choose the word from the box that is the best synonym for each group of words. Write the word on the line.

operation	foreign	defrost	whine	flexible
batch	forecast	banquet	dispute	plateau

1. from another land, alien, exotic   <u>foreign</u>

2. whimper, gripe; a wail, moan   <u>whine</u>

3. elastic, easily bent   <u>flexible</u>

4. group, bunch, amount   <u>batch</u>

5. large dinner, elegant meal   <u>banquet</u>

6. challenge, question; an argument   <u>dispute</u>

7. procedure, performance, activity   <u>operation</u>

8. melt, warm   <u>defrost</u>

9. foresee, envision, calculate   <u>forecast</u>

10. mesa, highland, upland   <u>plateau</u>

Vocabulary in Action

Our word *museum* can be traced back to the Greek word *Mouseion*. This Greek word meant "shrine of the Muses." In Greek mythology the Muses were nine daughters of the god Zeus. Each of the Muses was the guardian of a different kind of art or science. Many artists and writers thought that the inspiration for the greatest works came from the Muses. Today, we still call something that inspires our creativity a muse.

Part 2 Replace the underlined word(s) with a word from the box that means the same or almost the same. Write your answer on the line.

> paralyze   bacteria   museum   foundation   vapor
> desirable   glands   gauge   dungeon   easel

11. The headlights of the car seemed to <u>freeze</u> the raccoon as it was crossing the road. _____ paralyze

12. When the guilty prisoner is sentenced, he will be taken to the <u>underground cell</u>. _____ dungeon

13. To excel at math, you need a good knowledge <u>base</u> of fundamental facts. _____ foundation

14. The advertising agency will <u>judge</u> the success of its ads by asking you questions about the product. _____ gauge

15. Getting a ride to school on a rainy day would be <u>advantageous</u>. _____ desirable

16. We watched <u>fog</u> roll in off the lake this morning. _____ vapor

17. This mouthwash claims to kill the <u>germs</u> that cause bad breath. _____ bacteria

18. The room had a wooden <u>art stand</u> with finger paints for each budding artist. _____ easel

19. We lingered in the <u>showroom</u> of antique cars called "Streets of Yesterday." _____ museum

20. If the <u>organs</u> under your jaw are swollen, it could mean that you are ill. _____ glands

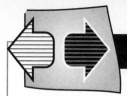

ANTONYMS

Antonyms are words that have opposite or nearly opposite meanings.

Part 1 Choose the word from the box that is the antonym for each group of words. Write the word on the line.

dungeon	dispute	whine
paralyze	foreign	batch

1. agree with; an agreement   _____dispute_____

2. cause to move, make powerful   _____paralyze_____

3. one, a single unit, sole   _____batch_____

4. low, quiet humming noise   _____whine_____

5. place of freedom   _____dungeon_____

6. domestic, native, of one's country   _____foreign_____

Part 2 Replace the underlined word with a word from the box that means the opposite or almost the opposite. Write your answer on the line.

foundation	plateau	desirable
defrost	flexible	banquet

7. There's a view of the mountains from this <u>valley</u>. _____plateau_____

8. We celebrated the end of the football season with a <u>snack</u> in the school cafeteria. _____banquet_____

9. Mom is usually very <u>firm</u> in her curfew hours. _____flexible_____

10. As Ruben read the menu, he thought the asparagus with cheese was <u>unappealing</u>. _____desirable_____

11. Take the package of vegetables out of the grocery bag and <u>freeze</u> it. _____defrost_____

12. The earthquake did no damage to the walls, but the <u>roof</u> is cracked.

foundation

WORD STUDY

Suffixes Use the words in the box below to answer the questions.

skyward	backward	homeward
upward	downward	westward

1. What two words in the box are opposites?

upward   downward

2. How would you describe the path of rockets, airplanes, and birds?

skyward

3. Which direction is opposite of going east? _____ westward _____

4. Where are you likely to travel at the end of the day?

homeward

5. When you count from 10 to 1, in which direction are you counting?

backward

CHALLENGE WORDS

Word Learning—Challenge!

Study the spelling, part(s) of speech, and meaning(s) of each word.
Complete each sentence by writing the word on the line. Then read
the sentence.

1. economical _(adj.)_ avoiding waste; efficient; saving

This family-size box of cereal is more _____ economical _____ than the
small size.

2. **fathom** *(n.)* a unit of length equal to six feet, used to measure the depth of water

The diver swam down one ___fathom___ to the coral reefs.

3. **morose** *(adj.)* gloomy; sullen; glum

On days when I'm feeling ___morose___, I like to cheer myself up with a funny movie.

4. **perjure** *(v.)* to cause the voluntary violation of an oath; to swear falsely

If you tell a lie in court and ___perjure___ yourself, you will be punished.

5. **refuge** *(n.)* shelter or protection from danger or difficulty

An overhanging roof makes a good ___refuge___ from the rain.

Use Your Vocabulary—Challenge!

Sub Thieves Imagine that you have seen a new movie about a gang of thieves who are caught trying to steal a submarine. On a separate sheet of paper, write a review of this movie using the Challenge Words below. Be sure to tell what the title is, what happens in the story, and what you think of the movie.

economical   fathom   morose   perjure   refuge

FUN WITH WORDS

An anagram is a word made by mixing up the letters of one word in order to spell another word. For instance, rearranging the letters of the word *moat* gives us the anagram *atom*. The letters are the same; they're just in a different order.

In the game below, you'll see an equation like this:

undone + g = a place you don't want to be ___dungeon___

The letters to the left of the equal sign are an anagram of one of the words from this chapter (plus one or two additional letters that are needed to complete the vocabulary word). The words to the right of the equal sign give you a hint. In the sample above, combine the letters from the word *undone* with the letter *g* and rearrange them. You should come up with *dungeon*, which is definitely a place you don't want to be! Write the vocabulary word in the blank provided, and you're done with that equation. Now try to untangle the anagrams below.

1. glad + n = something everybody has   gland

2. rap + vo = it's in the air   vapor

3. side + put = people taking opposite sides   dispute

4. leap + uta = don't leap from here   plateau

5. win + he = even if you don't win, don't do this   whine

6. store + df = an anagram that needs to warm up   defrost

7. painter + oo = how does this work?   operation

8. belief + xl = a highly bendable word   flexible

9. replay + az = don't freeze up!   paralyze

10. beadier + ls = you want these beads   desirable

11. craft + soe = it's a craft to get this right   forecast

12. hat + cb = not one hat but several   batch

13. seal + e = you won't see a seal use this   easel

14. grin + foe = give a grin to someone who is this   foreign

15. tribe + aca = a tribe of these is tiny   bacteria

Chapter 5   Level D

CHAPTER 6

WORD LIST

Read each word using the pronunciation key.

Group A

accuse (ə kyo̅o̅z´)
compass (kum´ pəs)
complain (kəm plān´)
disappoint (dis ə point´)
exaggerate (ig zaj´ ə rāt)
independence (in di pen´ dəns)
masquerade (mas kə rād´)
melody (mel´ ə dē)
sanitary (san´ i ter ē)
vacant (vā´ kənt)

Group B

campaign (kam pān´)
disarrange (dis ə rānj´)
echo (ek´ ō)
fault (fôlt)
fraction (frak´ shən)
haste (hāst)
horrid (hôr´ id)
justice (jus´ tis)
latitude (lat´ i to̅o̅d)
magnetize (mag´ ni tīz)

WORD STUDY

Prefixes

The prefix *re-* means "again."

react (rē akt´) *(v.)* to act back
replace (rē plās´) *(v.)* to fill or take the place of
recall (rē kol´) *(v.)* to call back to mind; to remember
rebuild (rē bild´) *(v.)* to build again
reuse (rē yo̅o̅z´) *(v.)* to use again

Challenge Words

compose (kəm pōs´)
inaugurate (in ô´ gyə rāt)
pallor (pal´ ər)
periodical (pir ē od´ ə kəl)
relent (ri lent´)

■ TEACHER TIP: See page ix for suggestions on how to use this page.

Read each sentence below to figure out the meaning of the word in **bold**. Use reasoning skills and the remainder of the sentence to help you. Write the meaning of the word on the line.

1. Brandy wants to **masquerade** as a vendor to get into the sold-out game.

to wear a mask or disguise; to go about as if in disguise

2. The song's **melody** reminded Kayla of a tune her dad used to whistle.

a sequence of single tones in a piece of music

3. Brittney forgot to set her alarm, so it was her own **fault** that she was late for swimming practice.

a mistake or an error; responsibility for failure

4. Ethan has no reason to **accuse** me of putting worms in his lunch box, but he still thinks I did it.

to charge someone with doing something wrong

5. Mason said he wanted just one bite, but only a **fraction** of it was left.

a part of a whole; not all of a thing

6. The smell coming from the garbage bag was so **horrid** that I held my nose as I carried it to the dumpster.

very unpleasant

7. Because Madeline worked the math problems with such **haste**, she made several careless mistakes.

a quick or hurried action

8. The new governor's speech had few new ideas. It merely **echoed** the ideas of the previous governor.

to repeat or imitate; to say or do what another says or does

9. The room was not **vacant**, so there was no place to hold the meeting.

empty

10. Peter is known to **exaggerate** about the size of the fish he catches.

to say that something is more than it is

WORD MEANINGS

Word Learning—Group A

Study the spelling, part(s) of speech, and meaning(s) of each word from Group A. Complete each sentence by writing the word on the line. Then read the sentence.

1. **accuse** *(v.)* to charge someone with doing something wrong

   Amy pointed to the man to _____accuse_____ him of stealing her sister's purse.

2. **compass** *(n.)* an instrument used to determine direction, having a needle that points north

   Use a map and _____compass_____ to guide you northward.

3. **complain** *(v.)* 1. to say that something is wrong or troublesome; 2. to find fault

   It does no good to _____complain_____ about bad weather.

4. **disappoint** *(v.)* to fail to satisfy one's hope or wish

   If the band fails to show up, they will _____disappoint_____ their fans.

5. **exaggerate** *(v.)* to say that something is more than it is

   That reporter tends to _____exaggerate_____ what he reports.

6. **independence** *(n.)* freedom from the control or help of others

   The rebels struggled for their _____independence_____ from the dictator.

7. **masquerade** *(v.)* 1. to wear a mask or disguise; 2. to go about as if in disguise; *(n.)* a costume party at which masks are worn

   The thieves plan to _____masquerade_____ as police officers.

   No one will guess who you are at the _____masquerade_____ party.

8. **melody** *(n.)* a sequence of single tones in a piece of music

   Adriana keeps humming that well-known _____melody_____ she heard on the radio.

9. sanitary *(adj.)* free from germs, dirt, and filth

The cleaning staff was praised for the _____sanitary_____ condition of the hospital rooms.

10. vacant *(adj.)* containing nothing; empty

The neighbors plan to build a park in the _____vacant_____ lot.

Use Your Vocabulary—Group A

Choose the word from Group A that best completes each sentence. Write the word on the line. You may use the plural form of nouns and the past tense of verbs if necessary.

My buddy Liam and I __1__ all the time about being the youngest in our families. So we decided to show our __2__ from our older brothers and sisters. We don't need them! Mom said we could camp out alone in the __3__ lot behind my house. "Camping is not __4__ !" sniffed my big sister, "There's no shower out there." Liam's big brother jeered, "You'd better take my __5__ so you can find your way home from the backyard."

   That night I heard an odd noise. I __6__ Liam of snoring like a bear. "You always __7__ ," Liam grumbled. He peeked outside. There was his big brother, trying to __8__ as a bear. We laughed and came out of the tent, whistling a happy __9__ . "Aw, gee," Liam's brother mumbled. "You weren't even a little scared." He tried to look __10__ , but I think he really was proud of us.

1. _____complain_____

2. _____independence_____

3. _____vacant_____

4. _____sanitary_____

5. _____compass_____

6. _____accused_____

7. _____exaggerate_____

8. _____masquerade_____

9. _____melody_____

10. _____disappointed_____

Vocabulary in Action

The first four letters in **masquerade** are pronounced just like *mask*, which one might wear as a disguise. This may help you recall that *masquerade*, when used as a verb, means "to wear a mask or disguise."

Word Learning—Group B

Study the spelling, part(s) of speech, and meaning(s) of each word from Group B. Complete each sentence by writing the word on the line. Then read the sentence.

1. **campaign** *(v.)* to seek election votes; *(n.)* a plan or series of connected activities done to get something

   "I will _____campaign_____ for the current mayor," said the volunteer.

   The mayor headed the clean-up _____campaign_____ and improved our community.

2. **disarrange** *(v.)* to put out of order

   A two-car accident is likely to _____disarrange_____ the headlights on both cars.

3. **echo** *(n.)* a repeated sound; *(v.)* to repeat or imitate

   Give a yell and listen to the _____echo_____ in these granite hills.

   Squawker, my parrot, will _____echo_____ any word you say.

4. **fault** *(n.)* 1. a mistake or an error; 2. responsibility for failure

   Who is at _____fault_____ for this broken window?

5. **fraction** *(n.)* 1. a part of a whole; 2. not all of a thing

   The sports store discounted the hockey sticks to a _____fraction_____ of the original price.

6. **haste** *(n.)* a quick or hurried action

   In their _____haste_____, they forgot their airplane tickets.

7. **horrid** *(adj.)* very unpleasant

   Is that _____horrid_____ smell coming from the chemistry lab?

8. **justice** *(n.)* fairness; rightness

   The judge's sense of _____justice_____ ensures the man will get a fair trial.

9. latitude *(n.)* 1. distance from equator; 2. freedom of choice or action

The _____latitude_____ of the island of Trinidad is on line with Caracas, Venezuela.

Alexis gave her employees great _____latitude_____ in making decisions for themselves.

10. magnetize *(v.)* 1. to make magnetic; 2. to attract or influence a person

Our science teacher showed us how to _____magnetize_____ a piece of iron so that it will attract metal filings.

Use Your Vocabulary—Group B

Choose the word from Group B that best completes each sentence. Write the word on the line. You may use the plural form of nouns and the past tense of verbs if necessary.

Drew Devlin's __1__ to become the next president of the United States was in trouble. Although popular in the Southern states, only a small __2__ of the voters in the North supported him. With only two weeks before the election, Devlin traveled in __3__ to the North to make speeches. He gave his speechwriters great __4__ in their choice of campaign issues. "Just get me the votes," he said. The main points the writers always covered were

- the __5__, troubling crime problem
- __6__ and fairness for all people
- correcting __7__ in the legal system.

Devlin __8__ the voters with his clear message of reform, attracting more and more of their support. Many of his statements __9__ the voters' feelings. Then just before the election, the polls showed that the order of candidate standings was __10__. Devlin had taken the lead.

1. _____campaign_____

2. _____fraction_____

3. _____haste_____

4. _____latitude_____

5. _____horrid_____

6. _____justice_____

7. _____faults_____

8. _____magnetized_____

9. _____echoed_____

10. _____disarranged_____

SYNONYMS

Synonyms are words that have the same or nearly the same meanings.

Part 1 Choose the word from the box that is the best synonym for each group of words. Write the word on the line.

sanitary	fault	justice	complain	magnetize
melody	horrid	accuse	disarrange	exaggerate

1. goodness, honesty, fair play   _justice_

2. sterile, clean, spotless   _sanitary_

3. guilt, blame, flaw   _fault_

4. magnify, boast, overdo   _exaggerate_

5. express displeasure, criticize, gripe   _complain_

6. persuade, fascinate, charm   _magnetize_

7. scramble, mix up, upset, jumble   _disarrange_

8. sickening, awful, gruesome, horrible   _horrid_

9. lodge a complaint against, blame, indict   _accuse_

10. song, ballad, tune   _melody_

Vocabulary in Action

An **echo** is usually caused when the waves made by a sound bounce off a flat surface. It is similar to the way light bounces off a mirror. Our word *echo* comes from Greek mythology. The nymph Echo was cursed by a goddess so that she could only repeat what other people said. She fell in love with a young man named Narcissus. Because of her curse, she could not explain herself. When Narcissus left, she hid herself and faded away until only her voice was left.

Part 2 Replace the underlined word(s) with a word from the box that means the same or almost the same. Write your answer on the line.

> vacant   independence   campaign   haste   masquerade
>
> latitude   disappoint   echo   compass   fraction

11. The candidate will <u>dishearten</u> his supporters if he withdraws from the race. ___disappoint___

12. Paul Revere rode with <u>swiftness</u> to warn of the approaching British. ___haste___

13. The Sonoran Desert may look <u>uninhabited</u>, but many creatures live there. ___vacant___

14. The money I earned shoveling snow is just a <u>portion</u> of what I expected to earn. ___fraction___

15. The language teacher instructed the class to <u>repeat back</u> each Spanish word. ___echo___

16. The tiny island government's <u>liberty</u> was assured by its strong army. ___independence___

17. In a <u>huge effort</u> to make the city beautiful, volunteers planted 12,000 flowers. ___campaign___

18. Whom did you dress as for the <u>costume party</u>? ___masquerade___

19. North, south, east, and west are marked on this <u>device to indicate directions</u>. ___compass___

20. Ahoy, ships at sea, please radio in your <u>position</u>. ___latitude___

ANTONYMS

Antonyms are words that have opposite or nearly opposite meanings.

Part 1 Choose the word from the box that is the best antonym for each group of words. Write the word on the line.

echo	masquerade	magnetize	accuse
fraction	haste	independence	complain

1. whole amount, complete object   _fraction_

2. said only once; differ from   _echo_

3. show oneself, reveal   _masquerade_

4. defend, pardon, stick up for   _accuse_

5. slowness, delay   _haste_

6. compliment, praise, approve   _complain_

7. slavery, lack of liberty   _independence_

8. repel, push away, repulse   _magnetize_

Part 2 Replace the underlined word with a word from the box that means the opposite or almost the opposite. Write your answer on the line.

fault	horrid	justice	sanitary
disappoint	exaggerates	vacant	disarrange

9. The water in this bottle looks <u>dirty</u>. Do you think it's OK to drink?
   sanitary

10. Whenever Grandfather tells a war story, he always <u>understates</u> his role in the victory. _exaggerates_

11. When you serve lima beans, you <u>please</u> everyone in the family.
    disappoint

12. There's nothing like the <u>pleasant</u> odor of an opossum living under your porch. ___horrid___

13. After the movie premier, the star was surprised to see a <u>crowded</u> theater lobby. ___vacant___

14. Take a moment to <u>organize</u> your drawer. ___disarrange___

15. Would you expect <u>dishonesty</u> to play a role in this crime? ___justice___

16. The <u>credit</u> for the look of our bedroom is my brother's, not mine. ___fault___

WORD STUDY

Prefixes Complete each sentence with a word from the box that means the opposite or nearly the opposite of the underlined word(s).

react	replace	recall	reuse	rebuild

1. Don't <u>throw out</u> that paper. I was going to ___reuse___ it.

2. After the tornado, the homeowners decided to <u>tear down</u> the damaged house and ___rebuild___ it.

3. I wish I could <u>forget</u> the worst game of my life, but actually I ___recall___ the game perfectly.

4. Should we buy more cereal to ___replace___ what we used or leave the pantry shelf <u>empty</u>?

5. <u>Ignore</u> the jeers of the other team's fans because if you ___react___, they will yell louder.

CHALLENGE WORDS

Word Learning—Challenge!

Study the spelling, part(s) of speech, and meaning(s) of each word.
Complete each sentence by writing the word on the line. Then read the
sentence.

1. compose *(v.)* 1. to make up; 2. to form by putting together; 3. to make
calm

Didn't Beethoven _____compose_____ nine symphonies?

2. inaugurate *(v.)* 1. to install in office with a ceremony; 2. to bring about
the beginning of with a ceremony

I believe that we _____inaugurate_____ the president in January.

3. pallor *(n.)* 1. lack of color from fear, illness, or death; 2. paleness

From the _____pallor_____ on your face, I can tell you don't feel
well.

4. periodical *(n.)* 1. a magazine that is published at regular times; 2. not
daily

National Geographic is a _____periodical_____ that comes out every
month.

5. relent *(v.)* 1. to become less harsh; 2. to let up; 3. to soften

I'll _____relent_____ this time and let you stay out later.

Use Your Vocabulary—Challenge!

My Magazine You are the editor of a new political magazine. The first
issue is coming out in two weeks. On a separate sheet of paper, write
a radio ad for your magazine using the Challenge Words above. Be
sure to tell what your magazine is about, the election stories you are
covering, and how much it costs. Try to make it sound so fascinating that
anyone hearing your ad will want to buy your magazine.

FUN WITH WORDS

Donovan discovers that a fierce storm has smashed his box of words. Help him put his words back together. Combine the broken groups of letters to form words and match each word with its definition. Each piece may be used only once.

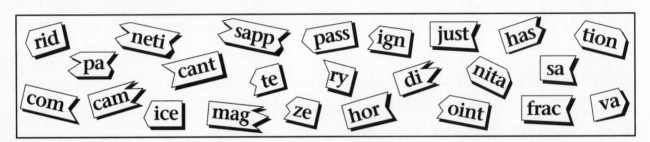

rid · neti · sapp · pass · ign · just · has · tion
pa · cant · te · ry · di · nita · sa
com · cam · ice · mag · ze · hor · oint · frac · va

1. A place that is empty is _____vacant_____.

2. This word stands for fairness: _____justice_____.

3. If you let someone down, you _____disappoint_____ that person.

4. People who rush are in _____haste_____.

5. If you can attract others, you can _____magnetize_____ people.

6. An area that is free of germs is _____sanitary_____.

7. This device points north: _____compass_____.

8. If you don't have the whole amount of something, then you have a _____fraction_____ of it.

9. Places that are very unpleasant are _____horrid_____.

10. A candidate seeking to get elected is sure to run a large _____campaign_____.

Review 5-6

WORD MEANINGS

Fill in the bubble of the word that is best defined by each phrase.

1. a sound that is heard again
   a. echo   **b.** foundation   **c.** vapor   **d.** whine

2. to not satisfy a dream or wish
   a. defrost   **b.** campaign   **c.** complain   **d.** disappoint

3. what you might need on a journey
   a. latitude   **b.** compass   **c.** masquerade   **d.** easel

4. to warm up
   a. defrost   **b.** exaggerate   **c.** disarrange   **d.** dispute

5. where objects are collected and displayed
   a. masquerade   **b.** gland   **c.** museum   **d.** compass

6. spotlessly clean
   a. horrid   **b.** vacant   **c.** foreign   **d.** sanitary

7. an angry argument
   a. fraction   **b.** independence   **c.** dispute   **d.** melody

8. to tell what's going to happen
   a. magnetize   **b.** disarrange   **c.** forecast   **d.** complain

9. can be seen only with a microscope
   a. bacteria   **b.** banquet   **c.** justice   **d.** dungeon

10. used to measure
   a. echo   **b.** gauge   **c.** compass   **d.** easel

11. having space available
   a. sanitary   **b.** horrid   **c.** vacant   **d.** flexible

12. an underground prison
   a. museum   **b.** dungeon   **c.** plateau   **d.** masquerade

13. a bunch of something
   a. echo   **b.** batch   **c.** melody   **d.** latitude

14. to cry in a childish way
   a. whine   **b.** disappoint   **c.** accuse   **d.** dispute

15. very bad
   a. vacant   **b.** desirable   **c.** horrid   **d.** sanitary

SENTENCE COMPLETION

Choose the word from Part 1 that best completes each of the following sentences. Write the word in the blank. Then do the same for Part 2. You will not use all the words.

Part 1

> paralyzed   masquerade   flexible   melody
>
> desirable   complained   exaggerated   plateau

1. Certain types of cacti cannot survive on a valley floor and can only grow high on a(n) ____plateau____.

2. After ten years of gymnastics lessons, Ryan was so ____flexible____ that he could touch the back of his head with his toes.

3. I found the ____melody____ catchy, but the song's lyrics bored me.

4. When I honked the horn, the dog became ____paralyzed____ with fear, and his owner had to carry him away.

5. I ____complained____ when I saw that my sister got more cake than I did.

Part 2

> foreign   horrid   fault   campaign
>
> magnetize   operation   justice   haste

6. The Spartans' military ____campaign____ was so well planned that they won the war within weeks.

7. Austin was supposed to bring the grill, so it is his ____fault____ nobody is eating hot dogs for dinner.

8. The visiting student's sense of humor was so ____foreign____ to me that I could not understand her jokes at all.

9. In their ____haste____ to reach the football game before kickoff, the Andersons accidentally left the car lights on.

10. Once I figured out that a battery controlled the ____operation____ of the clock, I easily fixed it.

Posttest

CHOOSING THE DEFINITIONS

Fill in the bubble of the item that best defines the word in bold.

Ch. 1   **1.** My best friend is the most **dependable** person I know.
         (a.) messy   **(b.) trustworthy**   (c.) kind   (d.) faraway

Ch. 3   **2.** The watch Grandpa gave me is very **precious** to me.
         (a.) old   (b.) cheap   (c.) pretty   **(d.) special**

Ch. 2   **3.** Garbage in a compost pile will **decay** over time.
         (a.) ripen   (b.) grow   **(c.) rot**   (d.) shrink

Ch. 6   **4.** Losing the camera was not Brianna's **fault.**
         (a.) error   (b.) accomplishment   (c.) idea   (d.) excuse

Ch. 4   **5.** Resources such as oil are becoming more **scarce.**
         (a.) plentiful   (b.) extinct   **(c.) rare**   (d.) common

Ch. 1   **6.** Pulling weeds can form a **callus** on your hand.
         (a.) cut   **(b.) hard skin**   (c.) rash   (d.) bruise

Ch. 5   **7.** The fierce pirate sent the prisoner to the **dungeon.**
         (a.) prison   (b.) auditorium   (c.) ocean   (d.) attic

Ch. 3   **8.** Dad hired a truck to **transport** our furniture to the new house.
         (a.) leave   (b.) lift   (c.) report   **(d.) carry**

Ch. 6   **9.** Being in an accident is a **horrid** experience.
         (a.) pleasant   (b.) dramatic   **(c.) unpleasant**   (d.) exciting

Ch. 2   **10.** I get an allowance so I can learn about **financial** matters.
         (a.) about work   **(b.) about money**   (c.) about wisdom   (d.) about art

Ch. 6   **11.** The new baby's room looked bright, cheerful, and **sanitary.**
         (a.) pretty   **(b.) clean**   (c.) dirty   (d.) colorful

Ch. 4   **12.** The mayor made an **objection** to the new law.
         (a.) argument   (b.) agreement   (c.) addition   (d.) promise

Ch. 5   **13.** The little fawn stood very still, **paralyzed** by our bright flashlight.
         (a.) stunned   (b.) frightened   (c.) angered   (d.) excited

Ch. 5   **14.** It was hard to **gauge** how much food to make.
         (a.) prepare   (b.) poke   **(c.) estimate**   (d.) feel

Ch. 2 **15.** When the hot sun came out, the water in the puddle **evaporated.**
    a. darkened   **b.** dried up   **c.** froze   **d.** spilled

Ch. 6 **16.** It does no good to **complain** about the weather.
    a. criticize   **b.** praise   **c.** dislike   **d.** enjoy

Ch. 1 **17.** Megan made a **pledge** to walk the new puppy every day.
    a. habit   **b.** story   **c.** promise   **d.** speech

Ch. 1 **18.** Everyone wants to be treated with **respect.**
    a. consideration   **b.** dishonor   **c.** glory   **d.** caution

Ch. 4 **19.** Victoria wants to learn to be a **surgeon** just like her mother.
    a. plumber   **b.** doctor   **c.** teacher   **d.** lawyer

Ch. 3 **20.** Until we got to know him, the new student seemed **bashful.**
    a. handsome   **b.** loud   **c.** smart   **d.** shy

Ch. 2 **21.** The strong wind made the fallen leaves **whirl** around.
    a. spin   **b.** drop   **c.** run   **d.** bounce

Ch. 6 **22.** I may have **exaggerated** the story of my touchdown a little.
    a. told   **b.** written   **c.** made larger   **d.** narrowed

Ch. 3 **23.** The American patriots fought for independence and **liberty.**
    a. honor   **b.** freedom   **c.** money   **d.** pride

Ch. 5 **24.** It took time for the ice on the car window to **defrost.**
    a. freeze   **b.** melt   **c.** harden   **d.** leave

Ch. 3 **25.** The two girls found a **satisfactory** solution to their problem.
    a. quick   **b.** useless   **c.** good enough   **d.** very bad

Ch. 6 **26.** Our team should not have **accused** the other team of cheating.
    a. blamed   **b.** arrested   **c.** avoided   **d.** fought

Ch. 1 **27.** Everyone liked the president's **sensible** plan.
    a. silly   **b.** boring   **c.** financial   **d.** reasonable

Ch. 2 **28.** William said I tripped him, but I was **innocent.**
    a. sleeping   **b.** not guilty   **c.** unhappy   **d.** quiet

Ch. 1 **29.** The boss praised Emma for being a **capable** worker.
    a. lazy   **b.** fit   **c.** pleasant   **d.** well-paid

Ch. 2 **30.** The workers built a **canal** to connect the two lakes.
    a. waterway   **b.** highway   **c.** railway   **d.** airline

USING CONTEXT CLUES

Use the word in bold and the sentence context to figure out the phrase that best completes each sentence. Fill in the bubble for your answer.

Ch. 6 **31.** You may hear an **echo** when you

    a. sing in a field.

    b. talk to another person.

    c. shout in a cave.

    d. dance in the wind.

Ch. 5 **32.** If you think something is **desirable**, you

    a. do not like its taste.

    b. wish you could have it.

    c. give it away.

    d. think it is ugly.

Ch. 3 **33.** When you look at the **galaxy**, you are

    a. looking down.

    b. looking into a river.

    c. always wearing dark glasses.

    d. usually looking at the night sky.

Ch. 5 **34.** If you visit a **foreign** country, you

    a. are probably far from home.

    b. are in your own neighborhood.

    c. are visiting your state capital.

    d. will see familiar things.

Ch. 6 **35.** A **compass** can help you

    a. tell the correct time.

    b. measure a long distance.

    c. find your way home.

    d. forecast the weather.

Ch. 3 **36.** When you pledge **allegiance**, you

    a. tell a lie.

    b. promise to be loyal.

    c. sing about your country.

    d. promise to pay back what you owe.

Ch. 4 **37.** A person who works as an **usher**

    a. shows people where to sit.

    b. buys and sells goods for a living.

    c. performs an operation.

    d. repairs cars.

Ch. 1 **38.** A person offers **hospitality** by

    a. curing a serious illness.

    b. not answering the door.

    c. refusing to share.

    d. inviting you to come in.

Ch. 2 39. If you lose a **molar**, you should visit

    a. a teacher.   **c.** a dentist.

    b. the police.   **d.** the dog pound.

Ch. 3 40. If you travel across the **equator**, you may be traveling between

    a. New York and Los Angeles.   **c.** the United States and Canada.

    b. North and South America.   **d.** California and Florida.

Ch. 2 41. An **obedient** pet

    a. follows your directions.   **c.** sleeps most of the day.

    b. chews up your shoes.   **d.** lives in a cage.

Ch. 1 42. An **industrious** person

    a. is always nervous.   **c.** talks too loudly.

    b. is usually lazy.   **d.** works very hard.

Ch. 3 43. A place with a good **climate** has

    a. a good police department.   **c.** nice weather.

    b. many landmarks.   **d.** independence.

Ch. 5 44. A person who ate a **batch** of cookies would probably

    a. still be hungry.   **c.** be very healthy.

    b. feel sick.   **d.** be very thin.

Ch. 4 45. When you **compare** two things, you

    a. measure and weigh both things.   **c.** spend time with both things.

    b. choose one thing or the other.   **d.** tell how they are alike and different.

Ch. 6 46. Justice has been done when

    a. a problem is settled fairly.   **c.** someone is arrested.

    b. someone is punished.   **d.** your team is the winner.

Ch. 3 47. Wild animals chase their **prey** because they

    a. need to have fun.   **c.** need to have food.

    b. want to have company.   **d.** want to get exercise.

Ch. 4 **48.** An **impatient** person would be unhappy if

(a.) the music was too loud.   (c.) the room was dirty

(b.) the food was burned.   (d.) the train was late.

Ch. 5 **49.** You could find a **gland**

(a.) at an antique show.   (c.) in a computer store.

(b.) in your own body.   (d.) in an office.

Ch. 4 **50.** The main job of a shoe **manufacturer** is to

(a.) wear shoes.   (c.) destroy shoes.

(b.) buy shoes.   (d.) make shoes.

Ch. 1 **51.** An award for **conduct** is given for

(a.) artistic talent.   (c.) good handwriting.

(b.) good behavior.   (d.) athletic ability.

Ch. 5 **52. Bacteria** are closest in size to

(a.) grains of rice.   (c.) specks of dust.

(b.) goldfish.   (d.) seeds.

Ch. 4 **53.** To see your **reflection**, you would look at a

(a.) mirror.   (c.) chalkboard.

(b.) scale.   (d.) watch.

Ch. 6 **54.** You would learn about **latitude** in

(a.) music class.   (c.) gym class.

(b.) English class.   (d.) geography class.

Ch. 3 **55.** You can see the **horizon** if there are

(a.) fluffy clouds in the sky.   (c.) very tall trees around you.

(b.) no buildings in your way.   (d.) many people with you.

Ch. 1 **56.** If someone **escorts** you, that person

(a.) hits you.   (c.) asks you a question.

(b.) sings to you.   (d.) goes with you.

Ch. 2 **57.** The state **capital** is

  a. a bird.   c. a flower.

  b. a letter in the state's name.   d. a city.

Ch. 5 **58.** One example of **vapor** is

  a. fog in the air.   c. ice on a pond.

  b. water in a river.   d. milk in a glass.

Ch. 4 **59.** A bathtub that is filled to **capacity** is

  a. overflowing.   c. half full.

  b. filled to the very top.   d. empty.

Ch. 6 **60.** If an object has been **magnetized**, it will pick up

  a. plastic toys.   c. iron nails.

  b. spilled water.   d. fallen leaves.

Ch. 2 **61.** If you feel a **draft**, you will be

  a. hungry.   c. scared.

  b. happier.   d. cooler.

Ch. 3 **62.** You perform an act of **charity** when you

  a. collect food for others.   c. buy new clothes for yourself.

  b. play in the school band.   d. do your homework.

Ch. 1 **63. Insulation** in your home keeps you

  a. dry during a rainstorm.   c. from running out of food.

  b. warm in the winter.   d. from going outdoors.

Ch. 5 **64.** An **easel** is often used by

  a. a doctor.   c. an artist.

  b. a mechanic.   d. a chef.

Ch. 1 **65.** An **eternal** flame will

  a. never go out.   c. be very hot.

  b. burn out quickly.   d. start a forest fire.

Posttest · Level D

Test-Taking Tips

Taking a standardized test can be difficult. Here are a few things you can do to make the experience easier.

Get a good night's sleep the night before the test. You want to be alert and rested in the morning.

Eat a healthful breakfast. Your brain needs good food to work properly.

Wear layers of clothing. You can take off or put on a layer if you get too warm or too cold.

Bring two sharp number 2 pencils with erasers.

When you get the test, read the directions carefully. Be sure you understand what you are supposed to do. If you have any questions, ask your teacher before you start marking your answers.

If you feel nervous, close your eyes and take a deep breath as you silently count to three. Then slowly breathe out. Do this several times until your mind is calm.

Manage your time. Check to see how many questions there are. Try to answer half the questions before half the time is up.

Answer the easy questions first. If you don't know the answer to a question, skip it and come back to it later if you have time.

Try to answer all the questions. Some will seem very hard, but don't worry about it. Nobody is expected to get every answer right. Make the best guess you can.

If you make a mistake, erase it completely. Then write the correct answer or fill in the correct circle.

When you have finished, go back over the test. Work on any questions you skipped. Check your answers.

Question Types

Many tests contain the same kinds of questions. Here are a few of the question types that you may encounter.

Meaning from Context

This kind of question asks you to figure out the meaning of a word from the words or sentences around it.

> The smoke from the smoldering garbage made her eyes water.

Which word in the sentence helps you understand the meaning of *smoldering*?

smoke	garbage
eyes	water

Read the sentence carefully. You know that smoke comes from something that is burning. *Smoldering* must mean "burning." *Smoke* is the correct answer.

Synonyms and Antonyms

Some questions ask you to identify the synonym of a word. Synonyms are words that have the same or nearly the same meaning. Some questions ask you to identify the antonym of a word. Antonyms are words that have the opposite or nearly the opposite meaning.

> The workers buffed the statue until it shone like a mirror.

Which word is a synonym for *buffed*?

> **polished**   **covered**
>
> **tarnished**   **dismantled**

Read the answers carefully. Which word means "to make something shine"? The answer is *polish*.

> When she feels morose, she watches funny cartoons to change her mood.

Which word is an antonym of *morose*?

> **dismal**   **agreeable**
>
> **happy**   **confident**

Think about the sentence. If something funny will change her mood, she must be sad. The answer is *happy*, the antonym of *sad*.

Analogies

This kind of question asks you to find relationships between pairs of words. Analogies usually use *is to* and *as*.

> **green** is to **grass** as _____ is to **sky**

Green is the color of grass. So the answer must be **blue**, the color of the sky.

Roots

A root is a building block for words. Many roots come from ancient languages such as Greek or Latin. Knowing the meaning of a root can often help you figure out the meaning of a word. Note that sometimes the spelling of the root changes.

Root	Language	Meaning	Example
audi	Latin	to hear	audience audible auditorium
bibl	Greek	book	bibliography Bible bibliophile
cred	Latin	to believe	credence creed incredible
dict	Greek	to speak	predict dictionary dictation
finis	Latin	end, limit	finish finally infinite
graph	Greek	to write or draw	autograph biography paragraph
scribe	Latin	to write	describe subscribe prescribe

Prefixes

A prefix is a word part added to the beginning of a base word. A prefix changes the meaning of the base word.

Prefix	Meaning	Base Word	Example
dis-	not, opposite of	like	dislike
mid-	in the middle of	air	midair
mis-	badly, wrongly	behave	misbehave
pre-	before, earlier	cook	precook
re-	again	paint	repaint
sub-	under	freezing	subfreezing
tele-	far away	photo	telephoto
un-	not	happy	unhappy
under-	below, less than	foot	underfoot

Suffixes

A suffix is a word part added to the end of a base word. A suffix changes the meaning of the base word. Sometimes the base word changes spelling when a suffix is added.

Suffix	Meaning	Base Word	Example
-able	able to be, full of	agree	agreeable
-al	relating to	music	musical
-ate	to make	active	activate
-en	to become, to make	light	lighten
-er	person who	teach	teacher
		run	runner
-ful	full of	cheer	cheerful
		beauty	beautiful
-fy	to make	simple	simplify
-ic	like a, relating to	artist	artistic
		athlete	athletic
-ish	like a, resembling	child	childish
-ize	to cause to be	legal	legalize
		apology	apologize
-less	without	hope	hopeless
		penny	penniless
-ly, -ally	in a (certain) way	sad	sadly
		magic	magically
-ship	a state of being	friend	friendship
-ward	in the direction of	east	eastward
-y	like, full of	thirst	thirsty
		fog	foggy

My Vocabulary in Action Dictionary

Categories: *Individual,*
Visual Learners

Create your own dictionary of vocabulary words. Take 14 sheets of white paper and one sheet of construction paper and fold them in half. Place the white paper inside the folded construction paper to create a book. Staple the book together on the fold. Label each page of your book with one letter of the alphabet.

At the end of each vocabulary chapter, enter the new words into your dictionary. Include the word, the definition, the part of speech, and a sentence. Each definition should be written in your own words. This will be a good tool to use throughout the year.

Vocabulary Challenge

Category: *Small Group*

Prepare for the game by choosing 15 vocabulary words from the current chapter. Write each word on a separate index card. On the back of the card, write the definition of the word. Place the cards on the floor, with the definition-side down, in three rows of five cards.

Three or four players sit facing the cards. The first player points to a word and gives its definition. If the player gives the correct definition, he or she gets to keep the card. If the player gives the wrong definition, he or she returns the card to the floor.

Players take turns until all the cards are gone. The player with the most cards wins the game.

Vocabulary Quilt

Categories: *Individual or Small Group,*
Visual Learners

Find one or two friends to help create a "vocabulary quilt," or create a quilt of your own. Write each vocabulary word from the current chapter in big letters across the top of a separate sheet of construction paper. Illustrate each word, using markers or colored pencils. As you finish, place the pictures in a quilt-like arrangement on a bulletin board. Leave the pictures posted in the room and allow the other students to "visually" learn their vocabulary words.

Toss the Ball

Categories: *Small Group,*
Kinesthetic Learners

Find four friends and sit in a circle on the floor. Your group will need a ball and a list of the current chapter's vocabulary words. The first person with the ball says a vocabulary word aloud, then quickly tosses the ball to another person in the group. That person must correctly define the word. If successful, that person says another vocabulary word and tosses the ball to another player. If the word is not defined correctly, the player must leave the circle. The game continues until there is only one player remaining.

For an additional challenge, say a synonym or an antonym for the word instead of a definition.

Synonym Partners

Category: *Large Group*

Write the current chapter's vocabulary words on index cards. Then write a synonym for each word on additional cards. Divide the class into two groups and give the words to one group and the synonyms to the other group.

The object of the game is for each student to find the appropriate synonym partner without speaking or using body language. The partners sit on the floor once they find each other. After all partners are found, each pair tells the class the vocabulary word, its synonym, and the definition.

This game may also be played using an antonym of the vocabulary word instead of a synonym. For a greater challenge, play the game using both a synonym and an antonym without using the vocabulary word.

Catch That Plate

Categories: *Small Group, Kinesthetic Learners*

Write the vocabulary words from the current chapter on slips of paper and place them in a hat. Ask the players to sit in a circle on the floor. Place the hat and a plastic plate in the center. The first player goes to the center of the circle, takes a slip of paper, reads the word, names another player, and spins the plate. The player whose name was called must quickly give a definition for the vocabulary word and then "catch the plate" before it comes to a stop. If successful, that player becomes the new plate spinner. If that player fails to catch the plate in time, the same plate spinner remains.

Vocabulary Egg Shake

Category: *Partners, Kinesthetic Learners*

Find a partner and write the current chapter's vocabulary words on slips of paper. Glue these slips to the inside of each cup section of an egg carton. Place a penny in the egg carton and close the carton. The first partner shakes the carton and then lifts the lid. The second partner must state the correct definition of the vocabulary word on which the penny landed. If successful, he or she must shake the carton. For a variation to this game, state the synonym or antonym for the vocabulary word instead of the definition.

This activity can be used for each new vocabulary chapter by replacing the vocabulary words with new words.

Vocabulary Search

Categories: *Small Group,*
Kinesthetic Learners,
ELL

Form a group of five students. Create alphabet cards from cardboard. Cut out 75 small squares and write one letter of the alphabet on each square. Make two alphabets plus several additional squares for each vowel.

Place the alphabet squares in two piles —with the same letters in each pile—in the middle of the playing area. Designate one person to be the announcer. The remaining four players break into teams of two. The game begins when the announcer says a definition, a synonym, or an antonym of one of the current chapter's vocabulary words. Then each team uses the alphabet cards to try to spell the word to which the announcer is referring. The first team to correctly spell the word receives one point. The team with the most points at the end of the game wins.

Vocabulary Baseball

Category: *Small Group*

Prepare for the game by drawing a baseball diamond on a sheet of paper. Be sure to include three bases and home plate. Write on index cards all of the current chapter's vocabulary words, along with their definitions. Find three friends and divide into two teams. Determine how many innings there will be in the game.

The first team at bat sends its player to home plate. The first player on the other team "pitches" a word to the batter by reading a word. If the batter correctly states the definition, he or she moves to first base. The player continues to move from base to base until he or she crosses home plate or misses the definition. When a player misses, the team gets an out. After three outs, the other team is at bat.

When a player crosses home plate, the team gets one point and the next player bats. The team with the most points at the end of the last inning wins the game.

Vocabulary Fables

Categories: *Individual,*
Visual Learners

Reread a popular fairy tale, such as "Cinderella" or "The Three Little Pigs." After you have finished reading the story, write your own version, using at least 10 vocabulary words from the current chapter. Make your new story into a book with illustrated pages and a construction-paper cover. Share your story with your classmates or with another class.

Comic-Strip Vocabulary

Categories: *Individual,*
Visual Learners

Prepare for the game by bringing to class some examples of comic strips from newspapers or magazines. Look over the examples for ideas to create your own comic strip. You can either make up new comic-strip characters or use existing characters. Fold a sheet of paper into six equal parts to create six frames. Use at least four of the current chapter's vocabulary words in your story. You should fill each frame with words and pictures. You might display your comic strip or share it with classmates.

Vocabulary Tic-Tac-Toe

Category: *Partners*

Prepare for the game by writing the current chapter's vocabulary words on index cards. Write the definition of the word on the back of the card. You will also need to create five *X* and five *O* cards. Place the vocabulary cards, definition-side down, in a stack. Draw a large tic-tac-toe board on a sheet of paper. Cover each square with a vocabulary card, definition-side down.

Work with a partner. The first player chooses a word and says the definition. If the player is correct, he or she removes the card and replaces it with an *X*. If the player is incorrect, the card goes to the bottom of the vocabulary stack and is replaced with a new card. Then the second player chooses a word and tries to define it. The game continues until a player has successfully made a "tic-tac-toe." This game can be played many times by shuffling the vocabulary cards between rounds.

Word Search Puzzles

Categories: *Partners,*
                 Auditory Learners

Prepare for the game by bringing to class examples of word search puzzles from newspapers, magazines, or books. You will need one sheet of graph paper and a pencil. Use the examples to guide you in creating a word search puzzle that includes some of the vocabulary words from the current chapter. On another sheet of paper, write the definitions of the words you included.

When you have finished your word search puzzle, exchange it with a friend. Take turns reading aloud your definition clues. Your partner must guess the correct vocabulary word and find it in your word search puzzle. Return the word search puzzle to the appropriate owner to check for accuracy.

Tell Me a Story

Category: *Small Group*

Find three partners. You will need two sheets of paper and a pen or pencil. Write all the vocabulary words from the current chapter on one sheet of notebook paper.

One person in the group begins creating a story by writing a sentence or two, using one of the vocabulary words. That person then passes the paper to the next group member. Each player is allowed to use only one vocabulary word each turn. The object of the game is to use all the vocabulary words correctly to form

a complete story. The story must make sense, and it must have a beginning, a middle, and an end. Ask someone to check your story for accuracy.

Vocabulary Role-Play

Categories: *Small Group,*
                 Kinesthetic Learners,
                 ELL

Find two partners. Pick 15 vocabulary words from the current chapter. Write each word on a separate small slip of paper. Fold the slips of paper in half and place them in a hat.

Each person selects a word from the hat. When it's your turn, take two minutes to develop a short skit about your word to perform for your partners. In the skit, you must act out your vocabulary word without saying the word. The first person to guess the word correctly draws the next word.

Jeopardy

Categories: *Small Group,*
                 Auditory Learners

Work with three partners. One player starts by giving the definition of a current chapter's vocabulary word. The other three players try to guess the word as quickly as possible. (They do not have to wait for the entire definition.) The first one to guess the word correctly gets to give the next definition. Keep track of who correctly guesses the most words.

Words in Context

Categories: *Partners,*
Technology,
ELL

Work with a partner at a computer. One person enters a vocabulary word from the current chapter. Then the second person enters a sentence using that word correctly. Take turns entering words and sentences. See how many you can complete in 10 minutes. (If you do not have access to a computer, you can write the words and sentences on a sheet of paper.)

Concentration

Categories: *Partners,*
Visual Learners,
ELL

Write eight of the current chapter's vocabulary words on separate index cards. Write the definitions of the words on eight more index cards. Shuffle the cards and place them facedown in a square with four rows of four cards.

Work with a partner. One person turns over two cards. If the definition matches the word, that player keeps the cards. If the definition does not match the word, the player puts the cards facedown in the same places they were before. The other player then turns over two cards. Continue until all the cards have been taken. The partner with the most pairs of cards wins the game.

A Word a Day

Category: *Large Group*

Each morning, write one of the current chapter's vocabulary words on the board. Encourage the students to use that word throughout the day. Keep track of how many times the word is used.

Hangman

Category: *Large Group*

On the board, draw a short line for each letter in a word. Read the definition of the word and have the students guess it by naming its letters. As each letter is called out, write it on the correct line.

Listen to This

Categories: *Individual,*
Auditory Learners,
ELL,
Technology

Some students, such as those who are not strong readers, will benefit from repeated listening. Record each vocabulary word followed by a slight pause and then its definition. Let individuals listen to the complete recording several times. Then have them listen to each word, stop the recorder, and define the word themselves. They can then listen to the definition to make sure they were correct.

Same or Opposite?

Categories: *Partner or Small Group,*
ELL

This activity will provide reteaching and reinforcement for students who need it. Prepare index cards by writing each vocabulary word on one side and a synonym or an antonym on the other side. Have partners or a small group take turns drawing the cards, reading the two words, and telling whether they are synonyms or antonyms.

Sentence Challenge

Category: *Individual or Small Group*

For reteaching and reinforcement, write a group of sentences, each using one of the vocabulary words. However, put the letters of the vocabulary word in alphabetical order instead of spelling it correctly. Challenge individuals or partners to figure out the word and spell it.

Find the Words

Category: *Large Group*

Encourage students to look for the current chapter's vocabulary words throughout a week. Remind them to look not only in books, magazines, and newspapers, but also on signs, in directions, and in ads. Tell students to listen for the words on the radio or TV. Have the students write down each word and where they saw or heard it. At the end of the week, count up how many times each word was found.

Be a Star

Categories: *Small Group,*
Technology

Have students work together in small
groups to write skits containing as many
of the current chapter's vocabulary words
as possible. Make a video of each group
performing its skit for the whole class.

Here is a list of all the words defined in this book. The number following each word indicates the page on which the word is defined. The Challenge Words are listed in *italics*. The Word Study words are listed in bold.